Mark

2.5

HOW I BECAME A YORKSHIREMAN

Also by Patrick Ryan:

HOW I WON THE WAR

HUBERT CALENDAR COUNTS HIS BLESSINGS

PATRICK RYAN

How I Became
a Yorkshireman

A SHORT GUIDE TO SOUTHERN IMMIGRANTS BY
A TIME-SERVING APPRENTICE YORKSHIREMAN

FREDERICK MULLER

First published in Great Britain 1967
by Frederick Muller Ltd., Fleet Street, London, E.C.4

Printed and bound by Cox & Wyman Ltd, London, Fakenham and Reading

CONTENTS

ACKNOWLEDGEMENT

This book is based on the series of
articles recently published under
the same title in *Yorkshire Life*.

□ □

CHAPTER I

THE FIRST LESSON

YORKSHIRE, LEST WE FORGET, is the largest county
in Britain, bigger than the Lebanon, Cyprus or
Jamaica, and bearing more people than Norway, Ire-
land or Bolivia. One-eighth of all England in area, ten per
cent of the English in quantity, but, by their own reckoning,
a hundred per cent in quality. A royal dukedom, eyrie of
king-makers, breeder of cricketers, Brontës, Captain Cook,
Delius, Guy Fawkes and Harold Wilson; eponymous to a
pudding and displaying within its borders, old cities bloody
in history, young towns harsh with industry, and bleached-
rock, sage-green landscapes of a peaceful beauty that would
relax even a dervish's eyeball.

And a people all its own.

The history of Yorkshire is the history of England. The
Romans marched up the Great North Road in AD 70, the
Saxons arrived around 547, the Danes came in 867, William
the Conqueror turned up in 1066, and I stepped out of a train
at Leeds City Station in 1954. Twelve character-forming
years have gone down the locust since that day of initiation

when, a raw immigrant from London, I first set eyes on the Black Prince and threaded my way among the naked lamp-bearing ladies of City Square. Keen to make a favourable first impression and anxious to show due reverence to the occasion, I was wearing my best bowler-hat, shortie Italian showerproof and grey suède shoes, and had given particular attention to the elegant rolling of my umbrella. I presented myself, in due course, before the desk of Mr. Josiah Micklethwaite, the factory manager who had been doomed by the gods at our headquarters to have me as his new deputy. He looked me up and down for a long minute, hoping, I think, that I might turn out to be a mirage.

'By . . .!' he gasped, changing his glasses for a better view. 'By . . .! Did you come through loading-yard in that la-di-da outfit and carrying that bloody umber-ella?'

'Yes, sir.'

'And right across factory floor?'

'Yes.'

'And through t'outside office into here?'

'Well . . . yes.'

He shivered, locked his office door and pulled down all the window blinds.

'By . . .!' he said. 'But it'll take you ten years to live this down, lad. Nobody in t'place'll take a blind bit of notice of you. They'll be thinking I've got lass wit' delicate air for deputy. I knew you were a right Southerner but I never reckoned on all this fancy-nancy.'

I had not, till then, realized that I was a Southerner. I had thought that England was populated by the English. I have since learnt, of course, that God, when breathing on the relevant handful of primeval dust, ordained that the country be inhabited, in strict order of merit, by Yorkshiremen, Lancastrians and Southerners.

It is quite irrelevant that people living in the south find no psychological need to refer to others as Northerners. Newly-arrived immigrants have lost their visas merely for thinking about such things. And it takes only a short sojourn in God's Own County to bring home to members of lesser breeds without the law that the misfortune of being born below Bawtry is a handicap in life second only to the curse of Cain. To Yorkshiremen in general and, as I soon found out, to Mr. Micklethwaite in particular, Southerners are the Englishmen Hitler had in mind, effete, soft-centred, a sort of latter-day Oscar Wilde, given to such decadence as wearing bowler-hats, fancy shoes and rose-coloured spectacles, and practising feminine weaknesses such as kow-towing to shopkeepers, describing spades as garden implements, growing mint in the garden, and carrying bloody umber-ellas.

At lunch-time on that first Yorkshire day, Mr. Micklethwaite smuggled me out down the fire-escape. It had come on to drizzle and I took my sensible gamp. He was so intent on getting me out of the back entrance unseen that he didn't notice I'd got the dread object until we were crossing the yard. As we came in sight of a group of our staff arguing by the gate, he pulled me suddenly back behind the cover of a lorry.

'That's the complete Shop Stewards' Committee,' he said. 'If they get sight of that umber-ella, they'll mark you down for life as a right jessie. It'll be strong-arm tactics all the way at Works Council meetings and everybody in the place'll be calling you Little Lord Fauntleroy or Sweetie Pie. Hide it, lad! For God's sake, hide it!'

'But where?'

'Stuff it under your coat.'

'It's too long.'

'Then get it under your arm and hold it against your leg like this. . . .'

He pushed the handle of the brolly up under my armpit like a foreshortened crutch. I clamped my arm straight down my side to hold it in place and to keep the protruding foot of ferrule hidden hard against my thigh. Stiff-legged as Long John Silver, right arm fixed rigid as a calcified Guardsman and keeping the brolly on their blind side, I hobbled up to the six shop stewards and was introduced to each in turn. I had, of course, to shake hands with my left paw, but hoped they would rationalize this handicap by thinking me an arthritic ex-Boy Scout. As I wooden-legged it through the gate, sweating cobblestones of relief, I could feel their twelve eyes running down my back like inquisitive lasers. But I finally won out for Mr. Micklethwaite. Nobody ever called me Little Lord Fauntleroy or Sweetie Pie. For the rest of

my career in Leeds I was known to one half of the staff as Peg-leg Pete and to the other half as Cripple Joe.

The rain began bucketing down, so, when out of sight of the factory, I elevated my umbrella and offered its shelter to Mr. Micklethwaite. He shied away as if I had come at him with a cobra. I learnt then that no matter how vocal he may be in doubting the masculinity of its bearer, there is nothing so puts the fear of God up a Yorkshireman as an open umbrella. When it rains in the Ridings, experience has taught me, frail women raise brollies, old men take taxis, but red-blooded Yorkshiremen just get wet. A Yorkshireman is more afraid of being seen by his neighbours with an open umbrella than with another woman. Mr. Micklethwaite walked grimly beside me like a man exercising a leper, a full yard away from me and indisputably outside the cover of my portable wigwam.

'Take note,' his face silently proclaimed to his passing compatriots, 'that courtesy compels me to walk with this Southerner. But I'm indisputably walking out in t'rain. Let the heavens open, come the second deluge, I'll get soaked to the skin, brew my West Riding catarrh into bronchial pneumonia, shrink an inch if need be . . . But nobody'll ever be able to say in t' singing-room that Josiah Micklethwaite was seen walking down Headrow under no bloody umberella.'

I lowered my brolly loyally and Mr. Micklethwaite came beaming back to my shoulder. We walked together manfully on through the grey rain and here, with Niagara sheeting off the brim of my bowler and the negroid lions of Leeds Town Hall nodding approval, ended my first lesson.

□ □

CHAPTER 2

HOW TO BE A NEIGHBOUR

Down south in a London suburb, you could live out your life without saying two words to the people next door. When you die, after twenty years of sharing the same dividing-wall with him, your neighbour looks up as they carry your coffin down the path and says to his wife, 'Looks like they're having a funeral next door. Wonder who he was?'

I was once baby-sitting at a house in Surbiton when the television was struck by lightning. The whole family next door, husband, wife and four kids, watched inscrutably over the fence as I dragged the smoking box out into the garden, but nobody spoke a single word in comfort or advice, never mind offering to lend me a bucket of water.

I don't know if you perhaps subscribe to the belief that the best service a man can do his neighbour is to leave the poor perisher in peace. But I do know that you won't stand much chance of practising such a creed in Yorkshire. Up North, neighbourliness is a religious mania. A Yorkshire-woman would sooner be called a right Jezebel than a bad

neighbour. The removal van has barely pulled up outside an immigrant's house before half the street are out with tea-trays, information and curiosity.

'How d'you do?' said Mrs. Grewelthorpe, following our three-piece suite up the path with tea and girdle-cakes. 'I'm from next door that way. I've heard you've come up from t'South but I'll not be holding that against you. Speak as you find, I say, and doan't take your opinions off'n other folks' tongues.'

'Very kind of you,' I said, taking the tray.

'It's nowt. If you can't be a good neighbour then what can you be?'

She trailed me into the house for a closer look at the quality of my furniture, carpets and wife.

'I suppose you know,' she said, fingering our uncut moquette doubtfully, 'that you paid three hundred pounds over the odds for this house?'

'I thought it was cheap compared with London prices.'

'London's not everywhere, my lad. He did you for three hundred did old Popplethwaite. You were too eager by half. When I saw you whipping out that tape-measure on first visit and measuring up for curtaining, I knew he'd rob you.'

'Still,' I said, 'it's a very nice house.'

'Could have been if he'd looked after it like I have mine. Five coats of paint on my kitchen ceiling, three unders and two tops, and you could lie on t'floor and put your hair up in t'reflection.'

'Very handy,' said my wife. 'If you were drunk.'

Mrs. Grewelthorpe's mouth came over right Methodist.

'I doan't know as I'd joke about drink, lass,' she said. 'Not wi' all t'boozers we've got down this street. Especially them Crockerbys on t'other side of you. By! . . . but if I had a penny for every gin bottle t'dustman tells me comes out of their bin, I could buy myself Buckingham Palace, I could that.'

'We haven't met them yet,' I said.

'And it'll not be t'luckiest day of your life when you do. I'm right sorry for you living wall-to-wall with them Crockerbys and their radiogram on rock-and-roll half the night. And don't you nivver lend them nothing, lass, unless you kiss it good-bye for ever first. She's had my second-best clothes prop ever since her's broke in t'big blow four years ago and'll likely have it till Domesday.'

'Thank you for the warning, Mrs. Grewelthorpe . . .'

'Don't mention it. No more than one good neighbour should do for another. And, before I forget, I'd have them kitchen floorboards up if I was you. Old Popplethwaite was down there hammering around in those foundations all night before your surveyor came round in t'morning. But I'll not hold you up any more, lad, for God knows you've plenty on with this place. And remember, lass, if there's aught you want, just give me a shout over t'fence.'

When she'd gone my wife and I moved into the kitchen to test the floorboards with her stiletto heels. Then there was a 'yoo-hoo' at the back door and Mrs. Crockerby came in bearing another tray of tea and girdle-cakes.

'I'm the other half of your semi,' she said, 'and I thought you'd just about be ready for a cuppa.'

'It's most thoughtful of you,' said my wife.

'Not a bit of it, luv. If you can't be a good neighbour then what can you be? I see you're checking t'floorboards. And I doant blame you. If old Popplethwaite's not left you dry rot in them joists, I'll go to sea in a wheelbarrow.'

'I thought I'd just take a look . . .'

'And take a look at t'back wall of garage, and all. Come

home lit-up last Christmas, he did, and drove clean through
and out over t'flower-beds. Patched it up himself out of all
sorts and I reckon it's only held together by the grace of
God and top coat o' creosote. Did he say aught about t'back
bedroom?'

'Nothing particular . . .'

'I didn't think he would. Not exactly a selling point, I

suppose. Folks round here say that forty-five years ago, a
young woman crossed in love committed suicide in your
back bedroom. Some say she does a bit of a haunt, like, now
and again, but I don't go for it. D'you believe in ghosts,
luv?'

'I've never seen one,' said my wife. 'Not yet, anyway.'

'Nor me neither. I nivver see a ghost in all my life and
I'll be sixty-three if I see next Pancake Day. If you have any

trouble with ghosts, lass, you just let me know. I'll give them a right hard look and turnabout for their pains, don't you worry.'

'Thank you very much,' said my wife.

One right hard look from Mrs. Crockerby and Dracula himself would have been only too pleased to creep back into his sarcophagus.

'And let me know, too, if her next door t'other way starts acting up on you. I've nivver been one for saying owt against any of my neighbours, but don't you ivver tell Mrs. Grewelthorpe any of your business unless you're anxious for it to be blabbed all over t'street. She's got a tongue as long as Lent, she has, and no mistake.'

'I don't really think . . .'

'And she's a proper dismal jessie, too. Anybody has a bit

of jollification after half past nine at night and she's hanging out of her bedroom window moaning about how her old man's on early turn in t'morning. And whativver you do, lass, don't you nivver lend her nothing. They've got hands like grappling-irons for other folks' property have them Grewelthorpes ...'

She broke off as the front door opened and Mrs. Grewelthorpe came into the hall.

'Just come back for the tray, luv,' she said. 'Why, hullo, Mrs. Crockerby! Nice to see you looking so well, my dear.'

'And you, Ada,' beamed Mrs Crockerby. 'Coming to see our new neighbours are all right, eh?'

'That's right, luv. And if they're as good neighbours as we've been these last twenty-five years, they'll have nowt to worry about.'

'They'll not that, Clara. Friends and neighbours are something that money can't buy.'

'And there's nowt like Yorkshire folk for t'neighbourliness. Ivverybody knows that.'

'Love thy neighbour, the good book says, and we're not ones to be forgetting that in Yorkshire, are we, Clara?'

'That we're not, Ada. If you can't be a good neighbour, I always say, then what can you be?'

'What indeed, luv?' amened Mrs Grewelthorpe.

And, neighbourly duty well done, they went off, arm in loving arm, with their two tea-trays and left my wife and I standing in our bare kitchen and listening fearfully for the rustling of dry rot beneath our feet or the creaking of ghosts above our heads.

□ □

CHAPTER 3

HOW TO COVER THE HEAD

URING HIS OPENING DAYS in the West Riding, the male newcomer from London gets a strange feeling that either he has suddenly grown a couple of inches or Yorkshiremen are all a bit pygmy. Perhaps they're shrunken, he ponders, by the dark-grey rain or stunted by a lifetime's inhalation of carboniferous air. But after observing for a fortnight or so the strangely regular sky-line of male, evening bus-queues, he comes to realize that although God made Yorkshiremen just as high off the ground as Southerners, the tyke loses three inches in the hat. Whereas the Londoner gains false height from the dome of his bowler, the Yorkshireman, literally down-to-earth, carries no flattering airspace inside his national headgear, the flat 'at.

There is nothing so nicely points the difference between the North and the South as the flat cap. The metropolitan Southerner favours the precarious but decorative cupola of the bowler, a receptacle well-suited to carrying water, moulding plum-puddings, or catching mice, but singularly

ill-adapted to the secure cover of the scalp. The Yorkshireman, ever mistrustful of fancy-dressing, plumps for a purely
functional model, tailored strictly to the purpose of pro-
tecting the male cranium from meteorological misfortune.
Southerners, in general, are afraid of the flat cap, fearing if

they wear it that they may be mistaken for workmen. Only
landed gentry, professional golfers, peers of the realm and
Yorkshiremen have the natural aplomb needed to carry off
this most sensible top-dressing.

I must confess that I was a full month in Yorkshire before
I fully appreciated the perfection of the White Rose helmet.
I was walking down Headrow back to the factory after
lunch with Mr. Micklethwaite, and the breeze was blowing,
as usual, half a gale off Penyghent. As we crossed the open
plain of the Garden of Rest, the Buslingthorpe Silver Prize
Band blasted out 'Gems from Aida' on the temporary
bandstand. Whether their output added critically to the air-
speed or not, I have never been sure, but a sudden,

reinforced gust lifted my City bowler from my head and sent it skimming like a pregnant discus into the forest of sounding brass. A black flying saucer, it bounced off the leading cornet, and ricocheted among the oscillating trombones until a lucky slide-swipe laid it to rest at the feet of the French horn.

'By! . . . lad!' said Mr. Micklethwaite. ''Twere lucky it didn't land in t'euphonium or happen you'd never have seen it back. Nip up quick and get it. We've got board meeting in twenty minutes and can't wait till end of t'opera.'

The lunch-time audience of Leeds loiners applauded vociferously as, crouched like a shy hunchback of Notre Dame and apologizing to the conductor's knees *en passant*, I sneaked up the side-steps in time to the 'Entry of the Priests' and retrieved my truant titfa. As I reversed out again, a revengeful trumpeter lowered his post-horn and gave me a triumphal blast full in the left auricle. The shock-wave set my ear-drums popping like bubble-gum, space-man's vertigo set in and I tumbled down the steps to spreadeagle myself among the potted ferns in a flounder worthy of Norman Wisdom. The crowd took it that I was employed by the Buslingthorpe Silver as a surprise knockabout comedian and they encored rapturously as I picked myself out of the greenery and ran off in pursuit of Mr. Micklethwaite, who had beat a hasty retreat lest any of his compatriots should discover he was connected with me.

'Let that be a lesson to you, lad,' he said as I caught him up, 'and get yourself a proper hat to cover what brains the Good Lord gave you. Instead of that Burlington Bertie soup-bowl you've just been chasing up and down t'bandstand.'

He took from his pocket his own trusty flat hat and unfolded it for my admiration.

'A flat cap, lad, that's what you want up in Yorkshire.'

'We call that a cheese-cutter down South.'

'And I'm not surprised. Daft as brushes, the lot of you. Whatever you call it, that's the finest piece of headgear since King Harold's nut-cover with t'nose-guard went out.'

He put it on. Its grey tweed wings settled down about his ears and the peak jutted defiantly from his brow.

'A flat 'at is the ideal headdress. Adapts itself to the phrenology of any wearer, fits snugly over all contours, and stays put in tornadoes. Wind'll have to blow your head off your shoulders before flat cap'll forsake thee.'

Since I was just then engaged in holding down my balloon-ambitious bowler with both hands, I didn't feel like disputing the point.

'And the peak, lad,' he went on, 'keeps the rain off your face in winter and stops t'sun scorching your eyeballs out in summer. The side-boards keep frost off your ears, and t'band don't cut off circulation of blood to the brain like that undertaker's pudding-basin you've got there.'

'I've never felt anything wrong.'

'I'm not surprised. But many's the time, lad, that you've taken it off in t'morning and I've seen that red ring round your temples and wondered for a minute if Red Indians haven't held up your bus and given you t'bowstring torture.'

'It doesn't affect my brain adversely, sir, I do assure you.'

'That's a matter of opinion, lad, but nivver mind about it now. A flat cap has social advantages, too. Do you know of any other hat a man can wear comfortably in draughty theatres without obstructing the vision of those sitting behind him?'

'Well, not off-hand but . . .'

'And with all these beat groups about these days, it's right handy in t'singing-room at pub for saving a man from being knocked prematurely bald by the decibels bouncing off the ceiling.'

'I must admit I really hadn't thought about the indoor virtues of hats.'

'Outdoors and all, it's versatile. Capital for fanning fainting ladies.' He took off his cap and flapped up a draught that would have blown a woman clean out of her swoon. 'And equally good for beating off importunate dogs.' He slapped in vicious demonstration at his own heels. 'And when you've done wearing it for a bit, you can fold it up and put it in your pocket. Can you do that with your bowler?'

'I'm afraid it's just not made that way.'

'Not made for nowt but looking fancy-dandy, if you ask me. And shall I tell you t'last advantage of mine over thine?'

'What's that?'

'If you've got a flat 'at in your pocket, you don't need to carry no bloody umber-ella... Here we are, lad, Samuel Umpleby's, best flat-'at emporium in whole of Leeds. Just look at all that lovely headgear.'

He steered me towards the window of a hatshop just a few yards from the factory gates.

'I rather like that one there,' I said, 'that russet-and-grey check.'

'Aye, that's a right hard-wearing model.'

'Shall I go in and buy it?' I said, as the breeze whipped again at my bowler. 'I think I could do with a proper Yorkshire hat.'

'I don't doubt you could,' said Mr. Micklethwaite. 'With that vanishing chin, your face could do with summat to put a bit of Winston Churchill into it. But I doan't know as how you can buy a flat 'at like that one yet awhile.'

'Why not?'

'Because that's a proper Yorkshireman's 'at, that is. And you've not been up here five minutes. Later on, maybe, when you've got a bit of service in. When we can see what hopes there are of getting a real bit of Yorkshire into you. . . . But come on now, lad, or we'll be late for t'board meeting.'

He took me firmly by the arm and led me away from the temptation of the flat-hat shop and into the factory. But later that afternoon, impelled by Southern cunning and the memory of chill Northern winds on a thinly-covered scalp, I sneaked out to Umpleby's and bought, for secret use outside office hours, that full-peaked, russet-and-grey beauty.

□ □

CHAPTER 4

LEARNING THE LANGUAGE

THE FIRST DUTY OF ANY immigrant is to learn the language of the new land. This is not so easy in York- shire because, compared with the voluble Southerner, the Yorkshireman doesn't talk very much. Convinced by birth of the inferiority of anybody bred beyond his own borders, he finds no need for the continual support of his own voice. He spends much of his time in contemplative silence, a state of thoughtful trance which the newcomer must be careful not to regard as sleeping with the eyes open. His words tend to be few and to the point, and when he does speak, he usually speaks in proverbs.

To open my second month in Yorkshire and with the full weight of four weeks experience behind me, I delivered to a management meeting a ten-minute oration on how my London training told me the Leeds factory should be re- organized.

'By! . . .' said Mr. Micklethwaite when I'd finished. 'You're a right good yammerer, I'll say that for you. I thought you'd got t'needle stuck on gramophone.'

'I'm sorry, sir, if . . .'

'We have a saying up here, lad, that you might do well to think on. If tha knows nowt, say nowt, and happen nobody'll notice.'

'I see . . .'

'And nivver say nowt unless tha's summat worth saying, or there's money in the matter. Save your breath to blow on your porridge and if you've any to spare, put it by because you'll need all t'puff you can raise on your deathbed.'

'If I might just explain, sir . . .'

'By! . . . lad, but you're not starting your babbling brook again. Not this side of dinner, any road. A fool's tongue, they say, is long enough to cut his own throat. By! . . . but if you're at t'next meeting we'll have to have t'first-aid man standing by wi' tourniquet.'

That breathy and unfinished ejaculation, 'By! . . .' is the standard expression used by Yorkshiremen to convey astonishment at my achievements. Not 'By anything-in-particular!' but just a heartfelt, long-drawn-out 'By! . . ., without ever naming precisely what or whom they are invoking, in the manner of lesser races who take in vain the names of Jove, Jingo, or Jiminy. It may perhaps be that Yorkshiremen appeal silently to some esoteric god whose name is never revealed to anybody born outside the county. Or do they merely exclaim by nothing to indicate that their horror at Southern-bred behaviour is beyond the range of human expression?

Any new arrival in foreign parts expects to have to adopt a fresh vocabulary, replacing old words with entirely new ones. Yorkshiremen, however, add a more subtle hindrance to the outsider by retaining in their language old words from King's English, but giving them entirely new meanings, regardless of either dictionary definition or national

usage. It takes a long time for a Southerner to find out that
when his Yorkshire secretary says she is 'starved', she is
actually in need more of cuddling than feeding. How is
anyone bred to speak ordinary English to know that when
she tells him 'It's getting right thin', she is referring not to
her lovely figure but to the sharpening wind? Who, un-
blessed by clairvoyance, could deduce from the remark,
'Her cat ran through our backyard', that she is indicating
that the lady under discussion is her distant relative? Or –
may the good Lord help all Southerners – that she means
it's going to rain when she tells you, 'It's looking black over
our Will's mother's?'

Outside the office, I caught a nasty cold over 'braying'.
Carpenters and joiners were fitting some new runs of racking
in the stores. I went out to check progress but met the foreman half-way there.

'How are they doing on the racking?' I asked.

'All right,' he said. 'I just left all four of them braying
away.'

'Braying?' I said, umbrage rising because, in the South,
braying is what donkeys do, idle raucous chatter. 'Why
didn't you stop them?'

'Stop them? But I'm the foreman. I don't want to stop
the staff braying once they've got going . . .'

'Oh, don't you indeed,' I said dynamically. 'Then we'll
have to have a few changes round here. You just get back
down to the stores right away and stop everybody braying
in company time.'

Half an hour later, I had the Shop Stewards Committee,
four members of the Carpenters and Joiners Union, a
deputation of foremen, and the Welfare Officer all lined up
outside my office and kicking up such a din of Yorkshire
protest that Mr. Micklethwaite came out to inquire what

was up. And to inform me, in due course of explanation, that whatever 'braying away' may signify in backward parts of the country, in the West Riding patois, it means 'working like a black'.

The meditative silence which Yorkshiremen often prefer to the spoken word is not, as a Lancastrian canard would have it, a pose adopted to cloak an actuality of ignorance in an appearance of wisdom. It is a habit, I believe, which springs from the psychological influence of their national anthem, 'On Ilkley Moor Baht 'At'. The anthems of all nations, except Yorkshire, are couched in terms of bombast, self-congratulation and proprietary rights to the exclusive services of the Almighty. But the doleful ballad of York-shiremen sings no such vainglory.

It tells, you may remember, that if you venture hatless on to Ilkley Moor, you will catch your death of cold and have to be buried there; then the worms will come and eat you up, the ducks will eat the worms, your fellow-men will eat the ducks and, in so doing, will have eaten thee. It is, in my theory, the repeated chanting in childhood of this sad, cannibalistic tragedy that leads Yorkshiremen into the habit of silent contemplation of ultimate things. What point is there, lad, in babbling madly and boiling under the collar, in the face of the final truth that we must all, like kings and queens and chimney-sweeps, come to duck-meat in the end?

'I'm surprised, lad,' said Mr. Micklethwaite during my second month, 'that anybody out on t'factory floor takes ha'porth of notice of you. Nivver mind not speaking proper English, you seem feared of letting go with both lungs.'

'But you told me, sir, not to talk too much. If tha knows nowt, say nowt and . . .'

'But if tha does say owt, let people know you're there.

c

Don't mumble your vowels all cut-glass and china-lips like Auntie Maud wit' mouthful of pins and needles.'

Having mastered the Yorkshireman's vocabulary and understood his silences, an immigrant can still come a cropper over the length of his vowels. I had been bred in the South to shorten all my vowels to vanishing point, whereas the Yorkshireman gives them full value and rolls them like organ-notes from the cavern of his chest. The farther North you go, the longer grow the vowels, and it was up around Middlesbrough that I found my crowning, vocal misery in fudge. This is my favourite sweetmeat, and my heart leapt when I saw a succulent trayful of it in the window of a Tees-side sweetshop.

'Half a pound of fudge, please,' I said in my best cut-glass cockney, snipping the vowel sharp enough to cut Professor Higgins.

'Fudge?' said the shop-lady in puzzlement, as one opening conversation with a Martian.

'Yes, fudge. Half a pound, please.'

She brought her sister out from the back to see what she could make of it, and got me to repeat my order to her.

'Fudge?' frowned her sister. 'Ah doan't know as we keep that.'

From the shopful of people now waiting, they selected as possible interpreters, a clever child who had just passed his eleven-plus and an elderly lady who had once been as far south as Derby. 'Fudge . . . fudge . . .' I mouthed at each in turn, but neither could rightly say as how they'd ever heerd on it.

Everybody set to muttering the strange word to one another, in the hope that repetition might lead to understanding. 'Fudge-fudge-fudge-fudge . . .' the soft sound went rustling around the candy-trays as if we had a shopful

of genteel Red Indians. In desperation, I pointed to the expanse of my pale-brown desire resting in the window.

'That's what I want. There . . . fudge!'

'Ah!' cried the shop-lady, a great light breaking over her. 'Foooodge! Foooodge, looove! Then why didn't tha say so?'

'Foooodge!' echoed all the people. 'He wants foooodge.'

Grabbing my half-pound, I ran off into the street without waiting for the change and left the little shop booming, 'Foooodge . . . foooodge' as if they'd got Flamborough foghorn going in t'back room.

□ □

CHAPTER 5

HOW TO BE OWNED BY A
YORKSHIRE TERRIER

I WAS ASTOUNDED WHEN I saw my first Yorkshire
terrier. I had anticipated as canine representative of a
people so devoted to silence, brass tacks and spade-
calling, something more on the lines of a miniature mastiff
or toy bulldog. At first sight, any other dog in the Kennel
Club catalogue, except perhaps the chihuahua, would seem
a more appropriate mascot for Yorkshiremen than the
spring-heeled, living Beatle-wig that carries their county's
name. Looking like a lapdog, flitting about like a four-
legged sparrow and living eternally on the yap, the Yorkshire terrier seems fitter mate for a volatile Taffy than for a
taciturn Tyke.

On closer acquaintance with the White Rose hound-dog,
however, you begin to see how its characteristics qualify it
as a Yorkshireman's best friend. There is no waste material
about the specification of a Yorkshire terrier. Built as
economically as a bird, it is manufactured from minimum
bone, essential muscle and maximum grit. It can afford to

be among the smallest dogs in England because it is secure
in the knowledge that it represents the biggest county.
Bulldogs and boxers and bloodhounds have need to look
big and fierce to deter other dogs from attacking them
because, deep down inside, they're just softies who treasure
nothing so highly as peace and quiet. No outward appearance of bulk or ferocity is deemed necessary by Yorkshire
terriers since they are birth-convinced that everything else
on four legs is dead scared of them. Originally bred larger
for ratting, they now come into the ring at a fighting weight
of under five pounds. As their bulk decreased, their aggres-
sion increased, and their lives are now ruled by a compulsion
to set about any creature more than ten times their own size.

Like their human counterparts, once they've got their
teeth into anything they'll hang on doggedly through to
their own selfish ends, impervious to obloquy, back-handers,
or buckets of water. True to their geography, Yorkshire terriers also despise Southerners. While they pay some occasional
attention to the dialect commands of true-born Yorkshiremen, they steadfastly refuse to take a blind bit of notice
of anybody bred below Bawtry. And, as I soon discovered
after buying my daughter one named Jasper for her seventh
birthday, you don't own Yorkshire terriers; they own
you. Their mothers apparently teach them as puppies that
they are doing the human race a vast favour by gracing
our homes with their pedigree presences, and that bipeds
were put on this earth solely to provide terriers with dog-
lives of Riley and all canine mod. con.

We bought a member of the county breed during our
fourth month of residence in the hope that such when-in-
Rome submission would contribute later to favourable consideration of our Yorkshire naturalization papers. This hope
was singularly ill-founded since Jasper, in fact, almost got

me drummed publicly out of God's Own County. In addition to his inbred addiction to chasing alsatians, horses and dangerous bulls to Kingdom Come, he also cherished an ambition to be a sheepdog. I am not certain whether this aspiration stemmed from envy of the working collies in the dales, or from the optical illusion that, at a terrier's nine-inch eye-level, a sheep simply looks like a large white dog with peculiar ears. Whatever may have been its motivation, this Bo-Peep complex beat fortissimo in Jasper's breast and whenever we were out together in the wide-open spaces he would bring me sheep. Neither shouting, nor swearing, nor buffeting with my secret, russet-and-grey flat cap had any effect on him when he was heading for a round-up. Though sharp as Einstein normally at recognizing words with the faintest reference to food, that dog, when about his personal pleasure, couldn't comprehend his own name bellowed from six-inch range into his stationary ear-hole, never mind getting any messages when going hell-for-leather across Blubberhouses Moor.

As he scuttered at their heels, knee-high to a puff of wind and no more ponderous, the poor sheep used to hammer bug-eyed through the bracken, half-out of their skulls in the belief that they were being chased by a ball of barking mohair. During the standard periods of ewe-pregnancy, we were thus forced to spend our weekends at the bingo-haunted seaside, unable to risk going up to the beloved dales lest Jasper got loose on a rustling rampage. It was fortunately out of such dangerous season when he found his finest hour as a low-level Lassie and nearly engineered my extradition. I was peacefully watching a cricket match in a recreation ground in Nidderdale when he slipped his lead from my deck-chair and shot off to scour the near-by moors and collect his record bag, to date, of thirty-eight Black-faces. Yapping proudly to announce his triumph, he drove them down towards me in a shaggy stampede, crow-straight across the crowded park, demolishing *en route* two cricket matches, thundering apocalyptic over the putting green, smiting like Ghenghis Khan through the tea-garden and scattering maiden ladies and girdle-cakes into a milk-splashed purgatory of rose-bushes. As Jasper flashed past me like a scruffy electric hare, I flung my flat cap at him. He swerved not an inch from his herding but, neat as a tent-pegger, snapped up my hat and bore it on after his flock. Like woollen hippopotami the demented horde went surging across the paddling-pool leaving a wake of sunken yachts and skin-soaked children, and laying waste all the simple people's pleasures until they finally came to corral inside the fenced foyer of the Ladies Lavatories. This public powder-room was of Victorian design and it was the coin-in-the-slot turnstiles at the entrance that stopped the sheep. If those ewes had had a penny each, they'd have been going yet.

The proud sheepdog settled on guard and demonstrated his skill at keeping all thirty-eight of his flock pinned within their convenient pen, oblivious to the mêlée of hysterical, tea-stained women, some distraught that their offspring might be drowned, some struggling among the sheep to get out of the Ladies, and others, tight-lipped and desperate, pennies at the ready, trying to get in. Uniformed officials blew whistles and the Yorkshire crowd shook their fists in unison, baying for the life of the owner of the blasted dog. I was deeply grateful, just then, that Jasper never admitted to having any connection with me in public places. So I slipped in for safety among the multitude and, disguising my voice with foghorn vowels, joined in the rhubarb for my own blood.

'Gurr, garr!' I shouted, feeling it inappropriate to level

any specific insults at myself. 'Send for the police. There should be a law.'

Although park-keepers flapped him with their regulation caps with badges on, cruel women threw stiletto-heels, and dumb-friend lovers lured him with sandwiches, Jasper remained rigidly on duty and let not a single lamb get out of the Ladies until two police-cars arrived. Then, when the sergeant had unbuttoned his notebook and was bawling over his loudspeaker offering rewards for information leading to the location of said dog's legal owner, said dog left his post with his tail wagging proudly, sniffed me out from among the vengeful mob, dropped my flat cap at my feet and gave me the happy lick of Judas. I took off like Lyn Davies, straight through the paddling-pool and out of the park, with that Yorkshire terrier yapping joyfully at my heels, the sheep streaming after because they could think of nothing better to do, and the wild, wild women yelling in hue and cry that I be condemned to a fate worse than death and tethered, Brynner-bald and hatless, on the wormiest outcrop of Ilkley Moor. And I never saw my lovely russet-and-grey flat 'at again.

□ □

CHAPTER 6

HOW TO DRINK

'THE USUAL, ALBERT,' said Mr. Micklethwaite to the barman. 'And what'll you have, lad, a strong shandy?'
'I'd like a pint of mild and bitter, please,' I said.
'Come again,' said Albert.
'Mild and bitter.'
A chuckle ran round the Smoke-Room and heads wagged in familiar fun.
'Give it to him, Albert,' said Mr. Enoch Arkengarth, my chief's drinking crony. 'He's got to learn. He's only just come up from t'South.'
I took this northern badinage in good part, feeling gratified that Mr. Micklethwaite had asked me round for an evening at his own local. Albert came across to our table with a tray holding a pint each for my two companions, and two half-pints with a drinking-straw in each.
'Best I can do for you, sir,' he said to me. 'Half of mild and half of bitter. If you suck both straws at one go happen you'll get t'right mixture.'
'But I wanted both halves in one pint glass.'

'Oh! I see, sir,' said Albert with mock wonderment and the light breaking on him fit for the road to Damascus. 'You mean *mixed*. That's what we say up here. You'll nivver get nowt but two glasses if you go round Leeds asking for mild and bitter.'

The congregation joined in a communal round of laughter and then settled back to attack their own rations.

'Here endeth the first drinking lesson,' said Mr. Micklethwaite, tipping my two into one. Although my chief had ordered, Albert held out the empty tray in my direction.

'Custom of the Smoke-Room, sir,' he said. 'Anybody as asks for mild and bitter has to pay for t'round.'

The faces of my hosts were buried deep in their tankards, so I paid up, adding sixpence as a tip to ingratiate myself with Albert.

'Aaahhh . . .' sighed Mr. Micklethwaite gratefully. 'That's a well-kept drop of beer, that is. You nivver gets owt like that down your gullet in t'South, do you?'

'It's certainly very good beer.'

'All beer's good, lad, when it leaves t'brewery. It's how it's kept as counts. There's no bad beer. Just bad publicans.'

'God sends the grub,' said Mr. Arkengarth, 'and the devil sends the cooks. And same with ale. Bacchus sends the beer but Beelzebub sends the publicans.'

'And down South,' added Mr. Micklethwaite, 'he's got a right monopoly. By! . . . but I've been served some slop in London. Mild beer they called it. More like mild washing-up water.'

He took a swig to wash away the taste of the memory.

'I must admit,' I said, 'that the beer in Yorkshire is the best I've ever come across.'

'Of course it is, lad. And for why? Because up here we don't stand for any rubbish. If t'beer's not up to standard, push it back across t'bar. Tell 'em if you wanted vinegar you'd be down greengrocer's, not in pub.'

'They get down South,' said Mr. Arkengarth. 'what they deserve. Ivverybody's dead scared of complaining. And so t'publicans get away with murder. If any Yorkshire land-lord served the thin-lady's lager they dish up down South, we'd have his windows in right sharpish, I can tell you.'

'So long as it's darker than rainwater but not necessarily as tasty, Londoners sup it. And tek short measure and all. If anybody up here, lad, gives you a pint wi' a Southern collar on it, d'you know what to say?'

'No.'

'Ask t'barman, "Can you get a double whisky in that?" And if he says he can, tell him, "Then fill t'bloody glass up wit' beer".'

'Or ask him if he's just come back from Wimbledon,' said Mr. Arkengarth. 'And when t'daft jessie says "No" tell him "I thought you'd got tennis elbow right bad from t'tender way you're pulling that pump".'

'I'm sure I'll never find it necessary . . .'

'You will, lad, wi' your cut-glass accent. They'll try short measure on you t'minute you say "mild and bitter". Sup up, now, and we'll have another.'

Mr. Arkengarth ordered his turn and Albert set them up.

'This is a nice, comfortable bar,' I said, looking around at the maroon leather chairs and mahogany panelling. 'I must bring the wife here for a drink one night.'

My partners choked over their pints like a pair of asthmatic walruses.

'Your wife!' gasped Mr. Arkengarth, as though I'd said Hitler.

'A woman!' cried Mr Micklethwaite. 'You'd bring living females into t'Smoke-Room?'

'She likes a drink now and again,' I said.

'Mebbe she does. But she'll not be getting it in here. This is Men Only, lad, and don't you go letting in no loopholes. Last refuge in West Leeds from wittering wimmen.'

'I'm sorry,' I said. 'We don't have Men Only bars down South any more. It's mixed drinking everywhere.'

'Don't tell me, I've been in 'em. You can't smell beer for t'paint and powder polluting t'atmosphere, nor hear thisen play dominoes for t'yammer-yammer-yammering.'

'Southern pubs,' said Mr. Arkengarth sadly, 'are always packed solid with females. Anybody chucks a wild dart south of Bawtry and its odds on it'll finish up in a bosom.'

'It's the wimmen that ruin economic balance of t'evening, lad. Drinking nowt but shorts and fancy cocktails as mek you bring out folding money ivvery round.'

'And keeping stroke count of t'number of pints a man's drunk and reminding him at t'first moment of euphoria that he's mekking a fool o' himself. I've had some, don't you worry.'

Mr. Arkengarth's moustache drooped at the painful memory and they both descended on their new pints for nerve tonic. Albert held out the tray to me.

'Custom of t'Smoke-Room, sir,' he said. 'Anybody mentions women in here has to pay for next round.'

I paid up again and left him another sixpence.

'Eh, lad,' said Mr. Micklethwaite sternly, as soon as Albert was out of earshot. 'Don't you go doing that no more.'

'Doing what?'

'Tipping t'waiter ivvery round. You don't get no medals in Yorkshire by throwing your money about. Ivvery second round we tip 'em up here.'

'Keep 'em grateful but not rich,' said Mr. Arkengarth. 'Give 'em too much and they'll get right independent.'

'I'm sorry,' I said, 'but down in London . . .'

'I know,' said Mr. Micklethwaite. 'You tip all the time. Afraid of waiters and flinging brass around like water. But don't do it round here, lad. You'll spoil t'pitch for us as has to live here. Enoch and I reckon on doing another thirty years in this pub and we'll be nigh on a thousand quid out of pocket if you set up a tipping-every-time trend.'

At first, they were all for making me go up to the bar and ask Albert for my tanner back in case I'd established a precedent. But they let me off on my promise not to tip him when it came to my next two rightful rounds.

'And another thing that's wrong wi' pubs down your way,' said Mr. Arkengarth. 'They don't have no Singing Rooms. Southerners are all afraid of enjoying themselves in public.'

'Aye,' agreed Mr. Micklethwaite. 'Ivverybody sitting up on Little Lord Fauntleroy stools sipping ruddy cocktails wi' little finger stuck out posh. Nobody daring to speak above a whisper, nivver mind joining in a bit o' striptease and sing-song.'

'Like drinking,' said Mr. Arkengarth, 'in a well-furnished mortuary.'

'Perhaps we do take our liquor a little more genteelly down South,' I said. 'But, if I may express my own personal opinion, I'd like to . . .'

A sudden hush fell across the Smoke-Room and glasses were transfixed in mid-swallow.

'What did you say, lad?' asked Mr. Micklethwaite in a voice loaded with horror.

'I was about to say that if I may express my personal opinion . . .'

'Don't be daft, lad! You can't do that on your first night in t'Smoke-Room!'

'Why not?'

'Why not!' He looked to Heaven for guidance. 'Because it's just not fitting, that's why not. You've not got no seniority. During his first year in t'Smoke-Room, a man can listen to t'conversation of his elders and betters and speak up when spoken to. In second year, he can ask questions and hold opinions so long as he keeps them to hissen. And only in t'third year of residence can he open his mouth when he likes and express his own personal opinions.'

'Protocol,' said Mr. Arkengarth. 'That's what ivverybody's got to abide by. Protocol. And bring the same again, will you, Albert.'

Albert brought a fresh supply over.

'Excuse me, sir,' he said, hovering with the extended tray. 'Custom of the Smoke-Room, sir. Any junior member who expresses his personal opinion out of turn has to pay for t'next round.'

I dropped the exact amount of money on the tray and buried my shame in the comforting pint. The waiter hung around hopefully, rattling change and waiting for a tip. I lowered my tankard and looked him straight in the eye.

'On your way, Albert,' I said. 'I'm not flinging my brass around no more. I've been in Yorkshire long enough to know it's every other round up here, lad.'

As he shrugged philosophically and went back behind his bar, I looked at my two drinking teachers for kudos. Both, unfortunately, were blind to my small victory, out of sight behind turned-up tankards and lost in a world of Yorkshire-brewed bliss.

□ □

CHAPTER 7

LEARNING ABOUT CRICKET

I DON'T SUPPOSE YOU go much on cricket, do you, lad?' asked Mr. Micklethwaite, during my first summer in Leeds.

'As a matter of fact, sir,' I said, anxious to show him that he had a sporting deputy. 'I'm really rather keen. I've been a supporter of Hampshire as long as I can remember.'

'Wheer?'

'Hampshire.'

'Nivver heerd on 'em.'

'But we virtually invented cricket in Hampshire. The Gentlemen of Hambledon started the first club in 1790 and played their matches on Broad Halfpenny Down.'

'You might have invented it but you nivver learnt how to play it. That's t'trouble wi' cricket in t'South, too many ruddy gentlemen players as don't rightly know which end of bat to put in t'blockhole. How many times has your team won t'County Championship?'

'Well . . . Hampshire has never actually won the championship yet but . . .'

'But Yorkshire has won it twenty-five times. Twenty-five times.' He savoured the sound of his triumph and beamed in county satisfaction. 'And from t'way we're skittling 'em out just now we look like making it twenty-six this year.'

'Winning the championship isn't everything, is it? Hampshire have played some very entertaining cricket this season.'

'Entertaining? Cricket's not for entertainment! You go to t'City Varieties for entertainment, not to Headingley County Ground. No wonder you nivver win nowt down South. You just can't take nothing seriously.'

'But cricket's only a game, after all, and winning isn't . . .'

'Only a game! Cricket? Hark at him!' He fanned himself with a plastic menu to recover from the shock. 'By . . .! but it's little wonder we lost t'ruddy Ashes. Only a game, he says, just a bit of an entertainment like . . .'

To Yorkshiremen, as I started learning then and there, cricket is indeed neither a game nor an entertainment. Deeper than a tradition, more fundamental than a religion, a reverence for cricket is bred into their marrow and fortified in adult life by irresistible tribal tabus. West Riding babies in their cradles instinctively play a straight rattle and when a Yorkshireman dies and wakes up in heaven, he pulls the peak of his halo a bit further down over his eyes and says to the nearest angel, 'Eh, lad, and wheer's t'cricket pitch on these here Elysian Fields.'

Visiting anthropologists to this island are ever fascinated by our English summertime ritual in which fifteen white-clad mummers take up solemn postures in mystic patterns on a greensward, countermarch to and fro every six balls or so, and perform a continuous square-dance when dexter and sinister come into central duet. And our scrutators have little difficulty in detecting why this ritual has become an obligation of the Yorkshire way of life. Governed by rules incomprehensible to the foreigner, conducted with a minimum of spoken words, and requiring steady application over long, dull periods, cricket satisfies the Yorkshireman's taste for secrecy, silence and slowly grinding 'em down. As a sport in which patience, guile and tenacity of purpose pay the best annual dividends, it was tailormade to the Yorkshire character. In the South, they talk of a game of cricket; in the North, it's always a cricket match. A match, a contest, a battle of attrition in which all is fair within the law, and which is neither won nor lost till t'last wicket's gone down and, in Mr. Micklethwaite's philosophy, the last rule has been exploited.

'They've got a right good batting side have Fazackerley's,' he told our factory cricket team just before our second round match in the Hunslet and District Heavy Industrial Half-Holiday Cup competition. 'Their first four have all had trials down at Headingley nets and we've got neither t'spin nor t'speed to worry 'em. We've won toss, so we'll put 'em in first.'

'But if they're so strong in batting,' I interposed, 'won't that be a mistake? They'll be fresh and they'll get the best of the wicket.'

He gave me a long pitying look but made no reply.

'Now what I want you to do, lads,' he went on to the team, 'is to have the fast-mediums on bowling just short of a length and as wide of t'leg stump as they can get 'em. Nivver bowl on t'wicket at all, no slips, everybody out deepish to stop fours and keep owt they can reach down to singles.'

'But we'll never get them out that way, sir,' I protested as the match started. 'Nothing venture . . . .'

'We don't want to get 'em out. Each side gets forty-two

overs apiece and t'winner is one as makes most runs. We just want to keep 'em quiet for forty-two overs and see what we've got to go for.'

'But that's not sporting?' I said. 'That's just not cricket.'

'Not what?'

'Not cricket.'

'Don't talk daft, lad. Of course it's cricket. What d'you think t'lads are up to out there wi' bat and ball? Playing bloody rounders?'

'I meant that it's not in the true spirit of the game.'

'I don't know about no spirits, lad, but we're after winning Heavy Industrial Half-Holiday Cup, not playing la-di-da ladies tip-and-run down South wheer t'players are more worried about thickness of t'cucumber sandwiches than winning t'match.'

Our lads played to orders and Fazackerley's opening pair spent two and a half hours chasing balls that were too low to hook, too high to sweep, and too wide to drive. But they managed to amass a very useful 122 for 0 in their forty-two overs.

'Three runs an over'll see us home,' said Mr. Micklethwaite instructing our openers. 'Tek it steady and have a good look at t'ball first chance you get. Five years ago, Fazackerley's worked one on us wit' piano wire sewn into t'seam.'

Our openers took it very steadily; so did our middle order; and likewise our tail until, after thirty-seven overs, we were 52 for 9.

'Now you know the drill, Waldo,' said Mr. Micklethwaite to our last man in. 'There's just half an hour to go. Have you got on t'pad wi' broken straps and that collapsible batting glove?'

'Aye, boss.'

'Soon as you get in have t'sight screen shifted back and forth for as long as t'umpire'll stand. I've given two kids a bob to run up and down in front of it now and again so's you can refuse strike a few times. And don't forget to appeal against the light.'

Crippled snails could have beaten our number eleven as he crept to the wicket. Sir Bernard Lovell never asked for such precise adjustments of his radio-telescope at Jodrell Bank as Waldo demanded of the sightscreen at the Woodhouse Memorial Recreation Ground. After three balls his doctored pad came adrift and play was held up while a replacement was sauntered out. Half-way through the next over his left glove flew off his hand and a fresh one was provided at funeral pace.

'This really is rather stupid,' I said. 'We can't possibly win with four overs to go and seventy-one runs wanted. We're going to lose anyway so he might as well have a dip.'

'We've not lost till they've won. T'park gates have to be shut in twenty-two minutes and match'll not be legally finished if we've not had our ration.'

'What happens then?'

'Under Rule 29, t'game is resumed tomorrow night or t'first night possible thereafter as weather permits. Fazackerley's haven't beaten us till we've had forty-second over.'

'But it'll only take them five minutes tomorrow anyway.'

'It could rain.'

'Well then, the night after.'

'It could rain for forty nights and forty days like at St. Swithins.'

'Or,' I said sarcastically, 'it might be the end of the world tomorrow.'

'Aye,' he said, brightening at the prospect of going into eternity unbeaten by Fazackerley's. 'That's an idea an' all.'

But though Waldo filibustered most conscientiously, it was all to no avail and the last wicket fell in the fortieth over, and we lost by sixty-nine runs. Mr. Micklethwaite drove me home in grim silence.

'I'm so sorry we were beaten, sir,' I said as I alighted.

'Beaten, lad,' he growled. 'By ...! but you Southerners give up easy, don't you? I've got a list in my pocket of all their player's names and addresses and I'm going round in t'morning to check their eligibility at t'league secretary's office. We've got twenty-four hours under Rule 29 to register any technical appeal. I tell you, lad, we're not beaten yet.'

And we weren't. He found that one newly-employed member of Fazackerley's team had previously played for another firm in the first round of the cup and was therefore ineligible under Rule 12, sub-section 6. And doubt was thrown on the propriety of playing a wicket-keeper who had taken money seventeen years ago from a Lancashire League club for looking after their baggage. So Fazackerley's were disqualified, we won on technical appeal and, to Mr. Micklethwaite's unbounded delight, went on to win the cup at the end of the season. The only fly in his cricketing ointment that year was that Yorkshire only came second in the county championship. Hampshire, disregarding the damage they thereby did to my prospects of promotion and my future hopes as an apprentice Yorkshireman, rashly chose that year to come top.

□ □

CHAPTER 8

HOW TO TREAT WOMEN

THE MALE APPRENTICE to God's Own County early notes with admiration the gallant, rearguard action that Yorkshiremen are still fighting in defence of male supremacy. The South has long since fallen to gynocracy and female tyranny is as firmly established there as it is in the States. Only the Northmen continue the struggle to uphold the divine truth that it's a man's world. They didn't give in to William the Conqueror until he laid waste their land from the Humber to the Tees and they're not going to be ground easily under any latterday stiletto-heel. Dedicated historically to keeping their whippets nearer the fire than their women, the stalwart Yorkshiremen strive yet to keep the female of the species in that state of contented servitude to which it pleased God to call her. And, apart from soot and pregnancy, their main ploy in this holy crusade is Yorkshire pudding.

'By! ... lad,' said Mr. Micklethwaite as I pushed my portion aside at lunch in the factory canteen. 'You don't know what's good for you. There's nowt like Yorkshire pudden for keeping cowd owt and putting a bit of ballast in your belly.'

'I'm afraid I've never been very fond of it.'

'That's because you've nivver had it made right. Don't know how to mek it in t'south. Dish it up soft as your heads and flat as funerals. Pudden's never no good if it's not beat up for twenty-five minutes by t'arm of a true Yorkshire wumman.'

It is by fervently propagating this myth about its manufacture, and demanding the eponymous pudding at every possible meal that Yorkshiremen manage to keep their wives so docile. Beating themselves dizzy every day over the batter-bowl tends to soften the natural acerbity of women, the eternal whisking gives them tennis-elbow in their throwing-arm, and the vibrations breed enough headaches to keep them continually placid with aspirin. I am also reliably informed that secret vigilante patrols of volunteer Yorkshire husbands are out night and day on A1 picking off electric-mixer salesmen as they sneak over the border.

Wise to the cunning and patience of the opposite sex, red-blooded Yorkshiremen are ever on the *qui vive* for any attempt to lure them imperceptibly down the slippery slope to Southern male-slavery. They take their gallant stand on the traditional division of life's labours into Man's Work and Woman's Work. I learnt this one Monday morning when Mr. Micklethwaite asked how we were settling into our new home in Leeds.

'Very nicely, thank you, sir,' I said. 'Except that my wife can't find a window-cleaner. I had to spend most of Saturday after noon cleaning the outsides for her.'

'You did what, lad?' gasped Mr Micklethwaite, rearing in his chair as if he'd been slightly electrocuted. 'You cleaned t'winders?'

'Yes.'

'So's all neighbours could see you?'

'If they chose to look, I suppose . . .'

'If they could believe their eyes! By! . . . lad, but you were lucky there was big game on at Headingley. Else t'other husbands down your street'd have choked you wit' your own shammy-leather.'

'Why?'

'Because cleaning winders is Wumman's Work. And we don't want any of you soft Southerners coming up and giving our wives any ideas otherwise. Thin edge of wedge, that's what it'll be, lad. By! . . . but if you pamper that missus of your'n any more she'll have you in t'pinny and doing washing-up.'

'Not likely,' I guffawed bravely, not daring to reveal that I had been in such state of kitchen servitude ever since t'first day after t'honeymoon.

Man's Work, as I have noted after enjoying many evenings of Yorkshire hospitality, consists of such chores as putting on his slippers, holding down the armchair, struggling to the dining-table, turning on the television, going out, coming back, and waiting for his supper.

Woman's Work, to which no true-born Yorkshireman may put his hand without suffering, by tribal taboo, some loss of masculinity, covers such diversions as cooking, washing-up, unstopping sinks, getting the coal in, polishing shoes, and even to real die-hards like Mr. Micklethwaite, painting and decorating.

'I have a man in every five years, lad,' he said, 'to do place up from top to bottom. If she wants any fancy-dandying in between, that's Wumman's Work and she mun do it hersen.'

When in my seventh month in the Man's County, my London-spoiled wife laid out the paint-pots and announced that, action this day, she wanted her kitchen decorating, I decided that the time had come to assert my developing Yorkshiremanhood.

'Nay, lass,' I said. 'Think on. You'll have to do it yourself. Painting and decorating is Woman's Work. That's what they say up here.'

'Think on thasen, lad,' she replied. 'And remember we weren't wed in High Street, Pudsey. I married thee in t'Old Kent Road. And dost know what we say down there?'

'What?'

'Them as don't paen kitchint my, don't eat my dinner. So get braying, buster.'

She took our seven-inch distemper brush from out the sink and, with a ladylike flick, wrapped it wetly round my ear. I am never one to boast about my achievements but I must say that I got a lovely finish on that larder-door.

Besides eternally defending his male supremacy against female attrition, a Yorkshireman must also be meticulously careful that his autocracy is visible to his peers. There was no mint in our new Leeds garden, so I asked Mr Micklethwaite if he had a few roots to spare from his own plot. He couldn't have been more outraged if I'd asked him for marihuana.

'Mint!' he cried. 'You'll find no mint in my garden. Nor nivver will as long as I've breath in my body and strength in my fingers to lug it out.'

'Why not?'

'Because mint in garden means wumman's boss in t'house, that's for why. That's what we say in Yorkshire and I'll not be having nobody saying owt like that about me.'

'I'm sorry . . .'

'And so you should be. Mint in garden, indeed!' He shuddered like a vampire contemplating garlic. 'And don't

you go putting it round factory as you thowt Josiah Mickle-thwaite grows mint in his garden or I'll have you trans-ferred back to bloody London.'

They're dead right in Yorkshire, too, about gynocracy following the mint. All my married life our gardens have been running wild with the stuff. I thought of taking a stand on herbs this time and telling my wife that I wasn't growing any in Leeds. But I thought better of it after reflecting on the wristy flick she'd given that distemper-brush and wondering what lasting injury she might wreak on me with the flat of a spade. So I eventually smuggled some roots of mint up from the South in a false compart-ment built into our car. They flourished as rampantly as usual when I planted them, and both our Leeds-loiner neighbours took to watering their fences with weedkiller every week lest the dread herb crept through and dragged them down to my depths of masculine degradation.

□ □

CHAPTER 9

HOW TO SHOP

O NE OF THE PLEASANTER surprises for the Southern
visitor to Yorkshire is the service he gets in the
shops. To shop-assistants in London, a customer is
basically an importunate stranger who keeps interrupting
private conversations. If madam, their eyes say, can find
the dress she wants hanging on a rack somewhere and will
kindly put down the exact money, then good luck to her,
but for God's sake don't keep bothering me because I'm
doing my nails and talking to my friend Marlene. Or we
ain't got the paint you want, mate, we don't propose to
get it, and please get out of the light because I'm working
out my pools.

Southerners put up with such treatment because they
are congenitally afraid of making scenes in public. Yorkshiremen, however, labour under no such inhibitions. Bred from
the cradle to seek value for brass, they don't mind shouting
the odds to get it. They have thus kept their tradesmen
mindful through the centuries of the ultimate commercial
truth, that the man who pays the piper calls the tune. The

late Gilbert Harding, vociferous crusader against crummy
catering, undoubtedly learnt all he knew about belly-aching
in eating-places during the period he was a constable in
Bradford. On my first visit to that city, I watched spell-
bound in admiration, while a visiting gourmet from Ossett
sent for a policeman because he found what he claimed was
a rabbit's ankle-bone in his Hong-Kong Fried Chicken with
Bamboo Shoots and Water Chestnuts. And Mrs. Grewelthorpe, our next-door neighbour in Leeds, was fabulously
credited with having made the coalman retrieve half a ton
of Best Bright Kitchen Nuts from her cellar because they
were not, in her opinion, sufficiently superlative, lustrous
or nutty.

She appointed herself our shopping adviser and took
command of my wife soon after we arrived.

'I just thought I'd look in, lass,' she said, 'and put you
straight about tradespeople. By! . . . but you've got to watch
'em round here. Give 'em an inch and they'll twist you daft.
For t'butcher, go to Poppleton's. But collect t'meat yourself.
Don't let him send it or he'll lump in that much fat, t'joint'll
float about in roasting-pan like Noah's Ark in Deluge.'

'I'll remember that,' said my wife.

'Although, if you don't mind my saying so, lass, you look
as though you could do with a bit more fat on here and
there. I hope you're not one of them young wimmen as
starves just to be in t'fashion.'

'Not a bit of it,' smiled my wife, just at the end of six
weeks banting on yoghourt and fresh air.

'Back will trust and wait, we say up here, but belly'll do
neither. You'll find Birkenshaw's the best greengrocer.
Only watch he don't start giving you specky apples off
back of t'pile. Pick 'em out yourself off t'front and make
him hold bag open while you do it.'

'I'll try that . . .'

'And don't forget to keep an eye on Grabble, the fishman, and t'crafty way he sets his fancy kipper arrangement so's you can't see finger on t'scale. And if any of 'em lumber you with anything not up to t'mark, tek it back to 'em. Tek it back and get t'brass off 'em.'

'I'm sure I won't have to . . .'

'And if any of our tradesmen tries anything on you because they know you'll be a bit soft coming up from t'South, just you tell 'em you're Mrs. Grewelthorpe's next-door neighbour and they'll soon pack it in.'

Unfortunately for my wife, Mrs. G.'s overflowing neighbourliness drove her to take the initiative in putting this warning round.

'I know she means well,' bemoaned my spouse at the end of our first month. 'But there's really no need for her to tour round all the tradesmen and warn them not to try twisting t'new, skinny little blonde wi' la-di-da London accent because I'm her next-door neighbour. There's not a shopkeeper in the district who's bothered to remember my name. All the assistants just address me to my face as Mrs. Grewelthorpe's next-door neighbour. I'm making no progress in local society at all. And today the butcher's even sent up his written bill headed to Mrs.-Grewelthorpe's-N-D-N. I'm beginning to feel faceless. Another couple of weeks and I'll have lost my identity altogether.'

But our shopping instructor made up for consigning my wife to social oblivion by raising me to local notoriety. I was in Mr Crowther's ironmongery shop buying a pound of inch-and-a-half nails when she sailed in and planked a tin of yellow paint on the counter.

'Tek it back,' she snapped. 'And give me back my money.'

E

The lid of the tin had clearly been off and there were brush-drips down the sides.

'What's wrong?' asked Mr. Crowther.

'It's not same colour as t'first tin you sold me.'

'But it's jasmine like the first one. Look, it says so on t'label.'

'Maybe so. But it's a lie. That's not same shade as t'other lot. You can see difference on t'kitchen wall where I finished one pot and started t'other.'

'I'll change it for you.'

'You'll not. I don't trust your paint no more. Give me t'brass and tek it back.'

After five minutes fruitless explanation, during which Mrs. G. barked 'Tek it back' every time he stopped for breath, Mr. Crowther gave up and refunded her nine and eleven. She stopped at the door and pointed me out to the waiting customers.

'That's my next-door neighbour, that is. So don't go trying none of your tricks on him, Joshua Crowther.' She turned instructively to me. 'I've been dealing with him for forty-four years, lad, but he's not caught me yet. Not for t'want of trying, though. You've got to watch him, all the time.'

'Tek it back,' said Mr. Crowther in mimicry as she swept out. 'If ivver she dies and doctors do post-mortem, happen they'll find "tek it back" engraved on her heart.'

When I got home with my nails, I found that in his fluster with Mrs. G. the ironmonger had given me two-inch nails. With her example fresh before me, I returned to the shop.

'I'm afraid these aren't right.'

'What's wrong with 'em?'

'I asked for inch-and-a-half. They're two-inchers.'

Mr. Crowther put on his aluminium-framed glasses and took a good look at me.

'If I gave you two-inch nails, that's what you must have asked for.'

'I assure you I asked plainly for . . .'

'I hope you're not one of them smart-aleck Southerners as reckon we're all a bit short in the head up in Yorkshire.'

'Nothing of the sort. . .'

'Then why are you trying this tek-it-back trick first time off? How do I know you didn't deliberately ask for two-inchers so's you could imitate old Mrs. Grewelthorpe and mek me tek 'em back?'

'Aye . . .' rumbled suspiciously round the shopful of waiting patriotic customers. 'Aye . . . Southerners would an' all.'

'I had no such intention . . .'

'Old Mrs. Grewelthorpe, remember, was born and bred in Yorkshire. She's got her rights. Sixty-four years she's lived round here and tek-it-back's fitting for her. But I don't hear as how you've been up here more nor five minutes.'

The local clients growled chauvinistically.

'All right,' I said, admitting defeat. 'I'll keep the two-inchers. And I'll buy another pound of inch-and-a-half.'

'Just as you wish, sir.'

Mr. Crowther weighed out the nails and handed me the package. I proffered the money but he left my hand dangling in mid-air and picked up the package of two-inchers.

'Seeing as you're a new customer, sir,' he smiled, rubbing in his victory. 'I'll tek these back in their place.'

'Oh . . . thank you,' I said and turned for the door.

'Just a moment,' he cried. 'Mr. . . . er . . . Mr. . . . Mrs. Grewelthorpe's next-door neighbour. You've got three-pence change. The smaller ones are cheaper.'

He handed me the threepenny bit with the magnanimity of an alpaca-clad D'Artagnan returning his sword to a defeated opponent, and I ran through the ranks of rumbling loiners and out into the eternal, grey twilight of Leeds.

CHAPTER 10

□ □

LEARNING MORE ABOUT CRICKET

IF THE ANGEL GABRIEL landed, one summer's day, on top of Big Ben, blew the Last Trump and announced that it was the end of the world tomorrow, you'd never hear a word about it from Yorkshire newsboys. They'd just go on shouting the progress of the current Yorkshire county cricket match.

Charlie, the ancient newsboy who boomed all day outside my office in Leeds, certainly considered nothing else worth crying out loud. For paper-selling publicity he used the following standard repertoire of cricketing cries, all carefully phrased to provoke interest without imparting information.

'Yorkshire on the way now!'
'Three down for Yorkshire!'
'Yorkshire on the attack!'
'Yorkshire bid for victory!'
'Yorkshire fighting back!'

Yorkshire on the way now! is used when things are in the doldrums, during barren periods before play starts or when it is held up by rain. While gulled paper-purchasers claim it to be criminally misleading no one has yet tested its legality in a court of law.

Three down for Yorkshire! – the actual number is varied at will – indicates obviously that three wickets have fallen but cunningly fails to reveal whether Yorkshire have taken three of their opponents' wickets, or three of their own have gone down. The only way to find out is to buy a paper.

Yorkshire on the attack! may have a lusty ring of Agincourt but, in cold fact, it simply means that Yorkshire are in the field and their bowlers are bowling. Trueman may be flogged barefoot, Illingworth may be running up knee-deep in his own footmarks, the enemy may have amassed 412 for 0, but to Charlie, Yorkshire are still on the attack.

Yorkshire bid for victory! raises the blood of every passing tyke and may occasionally mean that his team has six wickets in hand and only forty to get in the last hour. More often, as he only finds out after he's invested his fourpence, it signifies that they've got half an hour to get the opposition's last nine wickets or that a daring declaration has left them 212 to make in sixty-five minutes.

Yorkshire fighting back! is my personal favourite. When this rallying-cry goes up, the initiated know that the White Rose is proper withering. Not even in Charlie's elastic philosophy can Yorkshire be on the way, on the attack, or bidding for victory. '*Fighting back*' indicates that, wanting 348 to win, they've recovered from 32 for 5 to 78 for 8; or, having made 104 in the first innings and followed on, they have lost their first three wickets for two leg-byes. But, no matter how pitiful may be his county's plight, to Charlie the enemy are never winning – Yorkshire are fighting back.

His only honest, unequivocal cry is 'Yorkshire do it

again!' which he delivers in a gloating crow at the end of a match to proclaim that Yorkshire have added yet another win to their monotonous sequence of victories. He never lowers himself, however, at any time during a match, to mention the name of the enemy county involved. Feeling as I bought my paper one night that eight months' residence gave me the right to speak up, I remonstrated with him about this unfair anonymity.

'Why don't you tell the truth now and again, Charlie,' I said, 'and shout, "Hampshire knocking hell out of Yorkshire"?'

'Who's that?' he asked, peering up from the depths of his two overcoats.

'Hampshire.'

'Wheer's 'Ampsheer?'

'Down south. Next to Sussex.'

'Ah nivver heerd nowt about 'Ampsheer. They your team?'

'Yes, As a matter of fact, I've been a Hampshire supporter all my life.'

'Hast tha now? Ah'm not surprised.' A split-turnip grin bisected his face and his lip-stuck fag wagged affably. 'Ah thowt there mun be summat special about thi all togged up in t'bowler-hat and umber-ella. 'Ampsheer is it, eh?'

He pronounced the name of my native county as if it lay somewhere east of Katmandu. I would have lightened his ignorance then and there about the cradle of cricket had not half the factory been queueing up behind me for their evening papers. So I left the lesson till a week later when Yorkshire played Hampshire at Headingley.

For most of the first afternoon Charlie gave a somewhat subdued recital of 'Yorkshire on the way now'. Suspecting that the long continuation of this non-committal statement

might hide some local discomfiture, I bought my first paper of the match and found, sure enough, that Gray and Horton were putting up a good stand for Hampshire and had made 135 for 1. When, around tea-time, the news-cry changed to a more confident 'Six down for Yorkshire!' I made further investment to find that we had slumped badly to 186 for 6. But Livingstone saw things through to respectability by the end of the day and the innings closed at 260.

Next day, Charlie opened his bawling once again with 'Yorkshire on the way!' He switched to 'Yorkshire on the attack!' for an hour or so while Sharpe was putting together 70 and pushing the score along to 84 for 2. When he turned suddenly to 'Four down for Yorkshire!', I knew something was up. A quick dash outside for fourpennyworth of newsprint confirmed that his heroes had slumped to 110 for 4. He perked up to 'Yorkshire fighting back!' as Illingworth stayed for a useful 35 and saw the score along to 171 for 5. But when he changed his tune to 'Five down for Yorkshire!' I smelt another rat and found in his latest edition that the skids were under his lot. The last five wickets went down for 9 runs and the innings closed before tea for 180, although Charlie never revealed to his compatriots that anything worse than 'five down' had happened to their team. Sainsbury, bowling slow left-arm spinners, had toiled all day to take 7 for 77 but, for all the mention Charlie gave him, he might just as well have gone for a haircut.

After the tea interval when Hampshire opened their second innings, he stuck hopefully to 'Yorkshire on the attack!' An uncertain note could be detected by the connoisseur as Gray and Horton once again worked steadily up to 102 for 2, but a jubilant switch to 'Yorkshire bid for victory!' had me panting first in the queue for the late night final. Trueman had turned spiteful in the closing minutes, taking three wickets for two runs and leaving Hampshire at the end of the day with 109 for 5 and only 180 ahead.

On the third day, Charlie opened cock-a-hoop with 'Yorkshire bid for victory!' and I couldn't do a stroke of work for worrying about my team until he dropped to the defensive after lunch and took up with 'Yorkshire fighting back!' The afternoon edition showed that Barnard and Ingleby-Mackenzie had got sensibly together and had put on 90 for no further loss and built up to a tidy 200 for 6.

'Look, Charlie,' I said, pushing the paper under his eyes. 'It's Hampshire that are fighting back, not Yorkshire. We're the ones who are getting on top. Why don't you be honest for once and shout, "Hampshire bid for victory"?'

'Because tha's not,' he said, producing the next edition and taking another fourpence off me. 'Illingworth's just got that Dingleby-dangleby bloke o' yours out for 60 and you've just declared at 203 for 6.'

'Which leaves you 275 to get.'

'And we've got nigh on four hours. Easy. Dead easy. Reckon t'openers'll do it on their own ... Here y'are! Yorkshire bid for victory! Read all about it!'

I was out there like a greyhound with coppers at the ready when, an hour later, he dropped down a notch to 'Yorkshire on the attack!' Shackleton and White were getting among them and they were 83 for 5.

'What d'you mean, Charlie,' I demanded. 'Yorkshire on the attack? You're on the desperate defensive if ever a team was.'

'We've still got Freddie there. He can hit that lot off hissen ... Yorkshire fighting back now!'

This change of cry was brought about by the small print

of the stop press which told that Freddie had belted up 37 before being run out at 140 for 8.

'Go on,' I said witheringly, 'give 'em "Yorkshire on the way now" and tell 'em it's a defeat they're on the way to.'

'We could still mek it,' he said stubbornly. 'There's still two to go.'

My Hampshire heart sank like a stone when I left the office that night and heard Charlie yelling, 'Yorkshire do it again!' at the full blast of his lungs. He avoided my eye as I bought the late night final and learnt, to my relief, that the last two batsmen had made a gallant stand of 4, Yorkshire were all out for 144 and Hampshire had won by 130 runs.

'Yorkshire do it again!' he crowed on. ''Ere we are now ... Yorkshire do it again!'

'Charlie!' I said. 'Really! That's just sheer false pretences. Yorkshire do what again?'

He grinned up at me from the depths of his three overcoats.

'Yorkshire do it again! That's right enough. That makes the fifth game we've lost this season. What you got against that? ... Read all about it! Yorkshire do it again!'

And I went off to the bus-stop and left him selling his papers like hot Yorkshire puddings.

□ □

CHAPTER II

HOW TO TRAVEL

THE ADVICE MOST frequently given by Yorkshiremen
to innocent children and ignorant Southerners is,
'By ...! But tha've got to watch 'em, lad.' I have
not thus far been able to establish the total body of people
embraced by the sinister Them, but I have gathered from
my various Yorkshire tutors that it includes shopkeepers,
women, coalmen, working colleagues, barmen, motorists,
pedestrians, kids, Londoners, and all forms of uniformed
officials, particularly bus-conductors.

Yorkshire folk, over-burdened with a sense of public
duty, seem to make a life-study of the intricacies of bus-
fares, the calculation of fare-stages, and the mental addition
of empty seats. And Mr. Micklethwaite was well up among
the leading omnibus watchdogs. My house in Leeds was
near his home and, for a while, we used to catch the same
bus. On mounting each morning, he would inform the
conductor exactly how many minutes and seconds his bus
was off schedule. Next, he would proffer his money with a
statement of the journey proposed and the calculated fare,

couched in the tones of Fred Hoyle challenging anybody to debate the Universe. Before taking his seat on top, he would carefully count the number of vacant seats. At the next stop, if the conductor's call to the queue agreed with his tally, he would sit glum and frustrated. But if there was a discrepancy, he was up on his feet like an objecting Perry Mason.

'Six only on top,' the conductor would cry from below.

'Seven!' Mr. Micklethwaite would bellow back. 'I'm telling you there's room for seven up here.'

'Six only, I said.'

'Seven. There are seven seats upstairs. If you did your job properly, you'd come up and count 'em.'

'Six only. I'm running this bus, not you up there.'

'Hitler rides again,' Mr. Micklethwaite would declaim to the approving passengers. 'They can give over looking for him in South America. He's got job as conductor wit' Leeds City Transport . . . Tek no notice of him you lot in t'queue down there. First seven of you come right up.'

'I'm coming right up myself,' the conductor would finally shout. 'And happen there'll be another empty seat when I chuck you off for creating disturbance on public transport.'

Up he'd come, there'd be an official recount, people would remind people that they were paid servants of the public, numbers would be taken on one side, names and addresses on the other, we'd all be ten minutes late for work and when the conductor went down to agree to 'seven upstairs', he'd find there were only five people in the queue anyway. And as the bus moved grudgingly off, Mr. Micklethwaite would shake his head balefully and advise me that, 'By . . .! but you've got to watch 'em, lad.' And the rest of the bus would nod sagely and second the motion with, 'Aye, but tha have an' all.'

In private, as well as public transport, the Yorkshireman sturdily asserts his sense of justice. No matter whether on wheel or on foot, he is ever-ready to stand up vociferously for the divine right of way of whichever mode of travel he may momentarily be using. I was in the ninth month of my novitiate when Mr. Micklethwaite took me in his motor-car to see a customer in Bradford. His chariot was a vintage Jowett and he drove it as if there were truly fifteen wild horses locked up under the bonnet. He gripped the steering-wheel as one holding back runaways and hunched forward in a bulldog crouch, the better to get his shoulders into the job. As we rolled down Cookridge Street towards Head-row, the lights were showing red against us, but they changed in our favour just as we reached them. A plump lady, who had already set one foot off the pavement to cross in front of us, made hopefully on her way. Mr. Micklethwaite hit the hooter in a blast that fluttered the pigeons down from siesta among the negroid wrinkles of the Town Hall and brought the lady up short and rigid as Lot's wife.

'Have you not got eyes in your head, woman?' he yelled as we swept by. 'Can you not see t'light's as red as your own nose?'

As we went on down East Parade, he glared at me like some latter-day Caligula.

'By . . .!' he exploded. 'What did you think she was, lad? One half of ruddy suicide pact? There's pedestrians up here ought nivver to be let out without leads.'

As we came round City Square, a cubical, flat-capped gentleman looked us full in the bonnet, waited till we were five yards from the zebra crossing and then stepped out on to it.

'Look out, Mr. Micklethwaite!' I cried. 'We'll hit him!'

But unmoved, my driver sailed sedately on, his foot never going near the brake.

'Bluffing,' he said. 'I knew he were bluffing t'minute I set eyes on him. He knew plain as eggs it were our right o' way.'

'Then why did he step out?'

'Just to see if he could mek me put all on for t'crash stop. Ruddy pedestrians are like that up here. All want to show who's boss o' t'road. By ...! lad, but you've got to watch 'em. Raving lunatics the lot of' em.'

'But pedestrians do have some rights on the road ...'

'Rights, lad? Who pays for t'roads, eh? Overtaxed, exploited motorists, not daft-headed jay-walkers. Seventeen pounds ten a year I pay for t'Road Fund licence and by gow! I'm going to have my money's worth.'

And he did all the way to Bradford, hooting like Mr. Toad and shouting his doubts about the sanity and legitimacy of anyone on foot who dared to incommode his royal progress. We parked the car and walked down to Forster Square, on the other side of which lay our customer. Although the traffic was hammering around in a fair imitation of Piccadilly Circus at rush-hour, Mr. Micklethwaite, neither looking to right nor left, nor slackening his light infantry pace, strode out on to a zebra crossing and plunged straight into the maelstrom of internal combustion, holding up a commanding hand for the mechanical sea to open in his path. Bus-drivers stood in rigor mortis on their brake-pedals, taxi-tyres screamed in agony, motorcyclists pivoted acrobatically above their petrified handlebars, and a coalman's nag reared up like Champion the Wonder Horse.

'Come on, lad,' cried Mr. Micklethwaite as I cowered
back on the kerb. 'We're on t'zebra. We've got right of
way.'

Bidding the traffic to hold on a minute while he went
back for his nervous Southerner, he returned to the pavement, and shepherded me out into no-man's-land.

'You'll have to stand up for yourself, lad,' he said, 'against
these maniac motorists up here. By ...! but you've got
to watch 'em. If you don't have a go they'll leave you on
t'kerb till Christmas.'

'But it's not right to dash out like this. How would you
like it if you were driving?'

'Driving? Have you gone a bit soft in t'head, lad, wi'
nervousness? I'm not *driving*. I'm walking. And I know
my rights. Roads was made for foot-walking, lad, and man

F

on t'two feet God gave him has right o' way over anything else on t'road.'

'But I thought you said in the car that . . .'

'In t'car? I'm not in t'ruddy car now. Come on, lad, or they'll be off again, the speed-mad devils . . . Hold it now, or I'll have all your numbers down t'cop-shop in t'morning . . .'

And as we crossed the road through a gauntlet of Yorkshire malediction, Mr. Micklethwaite hurled back at the drivers all the obloquy regarding their insanity and illegitimacy that he had lately tossed out at pedestrians. Sweating imperial pints of embarrassment by the time we got to the other side, I consoled myself that I had learnt another lesson. No matter what other dubious claims they make to championship, Yorkshiremen are undoubtedly the best drivers and the best pedestrians in the country. Simply because, in either capacity, they have to cope with Yorkshiremen in the other. And, in both, By . . .! but tha've got to watch 'em.

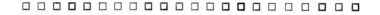

CHAPTER 12

HOW TO BE A SPORTSMAN

THE MAJOR ADJUSTMENT demanded of the sporting Londoner during his Yorkshire apprenticeship is that he rekindle the dead embers of his tribal pride. The remorseless spread of the Great Wen has obliterated ancient boundaries and nobody down there is quite sure where he comes from any more. But hometown patriotism still burns brightly in the North. The fire brigade stands by with hoses at the ready when Huddersfield play Halifax, and they board up the shop-windows when Dewsbury and Batley slog it out in the soot-grey mud. The holy tribal wars have been fought with the same neighbours for generations and not even the vendettas of the Mafia are pursued more relentlessly down the arches of the years.

All this, I learnt, as ever, the hard way. On first coming to Yorkshire, I fancied myself as a Rugby Union referee. Rugger in London is mainly played by geographically anonymous teams such as the Harlequins, Wasps or Saracens, and sporting nationalism rarely shows its teeth. But we were very hot on the True Spirit of the Game down there and were ever-mindful that Rugger is a game designed for hooligans and played by gentlemen. Which is probably why the All-Blacks keep beating the hell out of us.

The first Yorkshire game allocated to my control was a local derby between Gawford and Hogbury, two neighbouring villages in the slagheap foothills. They had been playing each other since about 1894 and as the crowd waited for the start, the older men were doing a Crispian and comparing their scars from past combats. As was my Southern custom, I visited each dressing-room in turn to exhort both teams to play the coming match in the True Spirit of the Game. Having now been in White Rose country for ten months I could make myself understood to the natives.

'Right, lads,' said the Gawford skipper when I'd done. 'Tha've heard what t'ref wants. And I want the same. I want thi all to go on t'field in True Spirit and bash t'bloody knee-caps of them ugly baskets from Hogbury.'

'And don't none of thi be forgetting,' added the vice-captain, 'what that Big Fat Cassidy did to our little Willie last year.'

My homily to the Hogbury team was punctuated by a rhythmic thudding as a prop-forward butted his head against a partition to harden it for the crunching to come.

'Like the ref said, lads,' their captain summed up, 'we'll have this game played in a True Spirit of Healthy Give and Take. Only make ruddy sure it's us that's giving it and them Gawford roughnecks that's taking it.'

'And remember they've got that Baldy Hughes playing this time,' said the full-back. 'Him what gave our Charlie false teeth three years ago.'

The crowd, unfortunately, didn't help the players to remember my message.

'Murder 'em, Gawford!' one half bellowed.

'Tear 'em apart, Hogbury,' the remainder cried.

And both factions joined in derogatory duet about the scragginess and pallor of the referee's knees. The teams lined up for the kick-off like thirty irritable Samurai and when I blew the whistle, the whole company met in one communal maul in a spot little related to where the ball had landed. As fast as I blew up and sorted things into proper order, the same indiscriminate mêlée set in again. When, on the fourth such occasion, the ball rolled out of the ruck unregarded to my feet, I realized that Gawford, thus far, were solely concerned with hunting down Big Fat Cassidy and putting the clog in as repayment for what he'd done to their scrum-half, Little Willie, in last year's game. The score was finally settled when Cassidy soared up like an overweight eagle at a lineout, to be cut off in mid-air by all eight of the Gawford pack, who bore him to the rails like pall-bearers and tossed him bodily to the crowd. As he fought his way back to the pitch through flailing caps and rolled-up newspapers, an old lady like Hilda Baker's small sister chased after him, belting his shoulders with her umbrella.

'Desist, madam,' I commanded. 'I must ask you to leave the field of play.'

'Ah'll teach the girt, fat ox to bray into my Little Willie,' she snapped. 'And I'll likely gi' thi a taster an' all, ref, if tha don't keep that Cassidy under control.'

Willie was four and a half feet tall, about the same across the shoulders and seemed to be built out of flexible, pink granite. Bent down, he was invisible on the far side of the scrum and, in gratitude for this God-given advantage, had dedicated himself to every known variety of Rugby villainy. Whatever it was that Big Fat Cassidy had done to him last year, Little Willie deserved it.

With Cassidy now paid off, the ball would probably have got back into the game more had not Hogbury decided to take up their three-year-old reckoning with Baldy Hughes for putting their full-back in need of artificial choppers. By half-time, after I'd blasted up for twelve penalties aside and the score was 6-all, Baldy had been given his deserts in toe-ends for that year, and grounds for at least four future vendettas had been registered in studmarks.

During the interval I addressed both teams on the True Spirit of Twickers and their captains assured me that, now last year's outstanding accounts were settled, I could look forward to letting the pea in my whistle fall asleep in these cond half. But its slumbers were shattered at the first scrum when both hookers suddenly dropped out of their sockets and took up private all-in-wrestling in the tunnel.

'I thought all the eye-for-an-eye stuff was over,' I said to the Hogbury skipper as we parted the mud-maulers.

'It was, ref, only their fathers both played hooker for their sides and our Albert's dad reminded him at half-time about the broken nose their Jimmy's old man gave him in 1948.'

The ball now came into its own for a while. Gawford scoring two tries and Hogbury notching another penalty to bring the score to 12-9 in the home team's favour. With five minutes to go Big Fat Cassidy emerged from a maul with the ball clutched to his bosom and a clear run for the line. Little Willie came for him only to be met by a hand-off which landed him straight into his mum's lap. Swearing wastefully, he bounced back into play, caught up with his enemy and tackled him from behind just as he dived over the line to score.

'Yaaoow!' yelled Cassidy, clasping his rear. 'He bit me, ref. The dirty little rat bit me.'

'Ah nivver did,' said Little Willie. 'Ah don't want food poisoning.'

Cassidy wanted to show me the teethmarks in evidence but I dissuaded him because there were ladies present. I would have sent Willie off but the crowd were baying for anybody's blood and his mother was swishing her brolly most viciously. Hogbury missed the conversion and the score was 12-all. From the kick-off, they drove quickly back into Gawford's half and would have scored again but for a gallant fall on the ball by Willie right on his own line. From the ruck, Gawford heeled, and the ball went out to the fly-half. He feinted for the open, then cut back inside, banging into me and knocking the whistle out of my hand, before returning the ball to Willie. The pass was slightly forward, so I groped in the mud to find my whistle and blow up for the infringement. Little Willie, meanwhile, doubled back across his own line and shot off down the centre like a jack-rabbit. He weaved through the forwards, swerved round his opposite number, side-stepped a covering wing-three, out-paced Big Fat Cassidy, kicked neatly over the full-back's head and gathered the ball again in full cry. With the crowd going mad and all Hogbury at his heels, he ran the complete length of the field, took off like a bird for the last few yards, grounded the ball triumphantly as two men hit him and rolled over to rest, out cold and unconscious in his moment of glory. All Gawford went up in pandemonium, frightening dogs as far north as Hunslet and setting avalanches flowing down all adjacent slagheaps.

I had by now found my whistle and, running up to where the men had left the ball, I blew an official blast and pointed back downfield.

'Scrum back on the Gawford line,' I commanded. 'That was a forward pass to Willie.'

'Scrum!' yelled the Gawford skipper. 'You can't, ref! We've won, 15–12! Greatest try in t'history of t'fixture.'

I blew again.

'The rules are the rules,' I said. 'That was a forward pass. I know it's disappointing, but you must take these ups-and-downs in the True Spirit . . .'

'Aye, and so must thi, ref,' he said. 'Tha'll be a True Spirit all right, any minute now, up on t'cloud wi' halo and brass harp if tha don't blow no-side and get thi skates on . . .'

The home crowd, the complete population of Gawford, were coming down the field like flat-capped Assyrians, the recovered Little Willie leading the way, his mum brandishing her brolly, vast men made of human teak waving variegated clubs, young children flourishing touch-flags and the whole community hell-bent after the liver and lights of the man who wanted to thwart them of their famous victory. I blew a long blast. 'No side,' I cried, formally completing my official duty, and beat it for the dressing-room, where I whipped up my clothes and carried straight on out through the back door to complete my toilette in the Gentlemen's Lavatory on Gawford and Hogbury Railway Station.

□ □

CHAPTER 13

LEARNING ABOUT BEAUTY

A S I DISCOVERED after plodding up and down two
or three of them, there is no lovelier tract of unspoilt
country in these islands than the Yorkshire Dales.
Residents of the county sometimes complain that its beauties
are sadly unappreciated by the British tourist. But they
might be better advised to swallow their pride since, so
long as the ignorant Southerner believes that the Northern
landscape is composed of chimneys and slagheaps, so much
the longer will the peace and solitude of high Yorkshire be
shared by those born to cherish it and fortunate immigrants
promoted from beyond the pale. To the newly-arrived
Londoner, accustomed to crammed roads and crowded
grass, the ever-changing face of the Dales is all delight. Eye-
muscles tensed by traffic-jams find balm in the spacious lower
reaches where the rivers flow wide and slow through pastures
so green that emeralds turn envious. As the land rises towards the Pennines, the rivers become mountain streams,
the sheep take over from the cows and clean winds blow
through diesel-haunted lungs. Higher still, as the dry-stone

walls displace the hedges, away up on the high fells where the moors sweep away to every horizon, olive and bronze and hazy-blue, and the limestone humps white against the sky, the peace, little brothers in the rat-race, it's wonderful. The big dome of space lifts the workaday yoke from your shoulders, the bowstring loosens about your temples, and the knots untie in your neck-muscles. A day in the Dales recharges the human battery and the rain-washed greens and silver-greys banish the bags from under your eyes more surely than any face-lifter's scalpel.

'Aye, lad,' said Mr. Micklethwaite when I regaled him one day with a full slice of the foregoing scenic hysteria, 'You'll nivver find nowhere wit' more beauty spots nor Yorkshire. Not even if you live to be hundred and four and travel to Timbuctoo. Have you been up Penyghent?'

'No, I haven't.'

'Then you've not seen nowt. Finest view in all Yorkshire from t'top o' Penyghent. You'll nivver see half as bonny down South, I can tell you.'

Like most other Yorkshiremen, Mr. Micklethwaite never wearied of eulogizing his country's beauties, praising its historic buildings, and suggesting places of interest that I simply must see. In the next few weeks, he had me up Penyghent, down Goyden Pot, through the Valley of Desolation, over Great Whernside, under High Force, and was bidding to get me airborne on Kilnsey Crag, when I discovered that he hadn't actually been to any of these passionately-recommended places himself.

When I taxed him with wilfully neglecting his own county, he said, 'I've seen 'em all, lad, on coach tours wit' bowling club. I don't necessarily have to set foot on 'em, do I? After all, I know 'em already. I were born a York-shireman.'

Mrs. Grewelthorpe, our next-door neighbour, insisted that my wife and I go to see Fountains Abbey, Riveaulx Abbey, Byland Abbey, the Brontë Museum, and York Minster. And borrowed the guide-books when we got back from each trip so that she could find out just what these gems of her own county's history looked like.

'I've nivver got time, somehow, like you, lass,' she said to my wife, 'to go gallivanting all over Yorkshire looking at famous places. But, of course, I were born here and that meks all t'difference, don't it? But, mind you, I've seen all there is to see in London. Everything, don't you worry, Buckingham Palace, t' Chamber of Horrors, Christie's house, the lot.'

One of the reasons why Yorkshiremen don't seem to have seen many of their own county's wonders is because they're so desperately worried about their roads. If you look along any moorland highway on a fine Sunday afternoon, you can see it's most faithfully guarded by loyal Yorkshiremen who are apparently dead scared somebody will pinch it. They therefore remain always on the alert, never taking their cars beyond the verge, and never placing their aluminium picnic chairs farther than twenty feet from the precious tarmac. The most conscientious road-guards never even get out of their cars, but sit in them all day, ostensibly reading their Sunday newspapers, but actually poised, watchful as any Welshman guarding his rainwater, to leap into action at the first sign of highway robbery. Man, woman, and motoring Yorkshire child all seem obsessed with the fear that if they stray away from the road for a moment, some villain will come along and roll it up. As a result, the only people you meet in the far depths of the Yorkshire Moors, walking across country on their own two feet, recklessly neglectful of the safety of the county's asphalt, are usually Southerners, Scotsmen, or other foreigners.

'If you've done Whernside and Penyghent, lad,' said Mr. Micklethwaite, as my first autumn in Yorkshire grew frosty, 'then you'll have to finish off t'Three Peaks and get yourself up Ingleborough before t'back end gets too bitter. It's nigh on a mile round t'summit and they used to hold horses races up there in t'old days. You can see Morecambe from t'top and that's summat, lad, even if it is in Lancashire.'

He set me off from Ingleton and it looked right black over our Will's mother's as I took the well-worn track out of town. As I came up over Storrs Common, the wind developed an iceberg tinge and soft needles of sleet did a world of good to my complexion. There was not another human in sight as I slogged up the slopes of the great whaleback, fond hopes of finish raised by each false crest as I climbed it, only to be dashed by another hump rolling beyond. When I finally came out on to the vast summit plateau, it was snowing thinly and you couldn't see Ingleton, never mind Morecambe Bay. But, as I trudged up to the shelter wall, I saw another climber already there and brushing the snowflakes off the mountain indicator. Surely, I thought, only a devoted Yorkshireman of highest degree could be up on Ingleborough in such unkindly weather. He looked as sturdily Yorkshire as Freddie Trueman, although not perhaps as broad in the beam. He was wearing a big, hairy flat cap, dalesman's knickerbockers, jacket of invulnerable tweed, and a pair of boots indubitably made for walking.

"Ow do, lad!' I cried in my best Yorkshire. 'By . . .! but Ah weer right starved cooming oop t'last lap. 'Ow art tha feeling thisen?'

'Perishing cold, mate,' he said in clattering cockney. 'Talk abaht flipping brass monkeys! I fought me lugholes had dropped off from frostbite coming over Simon Fell.'

'Stone the flaming crows, mate!' I said. 'And are you from the Big Smoke, too?'

'Born and bred in the Old Kent Road,' he said, 'but it's lovely country up here in Tykeland, ain't it?'

'Marvellous,' I said. 'Better'n round the old Elephant and Castle.'

With which he signified metropolitan agreement, and we sat down in the lee of the shelter wall, monarchs of all the snow and millstone grit we surveyed, in lone command of highest Yorkshire. And so we sat, two cockney apprentices on top of Ingleborough, sharing our coffee and wads, discussing all the horrible things that glazed matchbox-builders were doing to the Old Kent Road, wondering how old Henery Cooper was doing in the Thomas à Becket gym, and agreeing that if any Yorkshiremen want to hold horse-races on top of our mountain that day, they'd have to bring out their reindeer.

□ □

CHAPTER 14

LEARNING ABOUT T'LEAGUE

'HAVE YOU SEEN ANY Rugby up here, lad?' asked Mr. Micklethwaite, one wintry lunch-time.

'Quite a few games,' I said. 'And I've done a bit of refereeing these last few weeks.'

'I don't mean Union. Not t'boy's game. I was talking about t'man's game, Rugby League.'

'Rugby League!' I exclaimed, my amateur tongue barely able to pronounce that dread name which we are conditioned in the South to regard as the footballing Anti-Christ. 'I haven't watched any of *that*. After all, it's professional.'

'Of course it is. Proper professional. Not all under cover like your lot wit' people claiming taxi-fares from John o' Groats and finding money stuffed in their boots.'

'I never found any money stuffed in my boots when I was playing.'

'Maybe you weren't good enough. Where did you play?'

'Prop-forward.'

He pushed his glasses up his nose and took a longer look at me.

'Prop-forward? No wonder you nivver found quid-notes in your suède shoes. Wit' you up front, I bet your team needed Samson and Goliath in t'second row. You don't look thick enough through, lad, to prop up t'clothes-line, nivver mind holding up a full-grown hooker.'

Since this opinion approximated to that occasionally hissed into my scrum-tortured ears by collapsing hookers, I did not dispute the point further, but agreed to go with him to Headingley that Saturday to see t'man's game for myself.

'Who did you play for down South?' he asked as we came through the turnstiles.

'Old Fauntlerovians.'

'Old Boys team, eh? Well don't start coming over all Old School Tie up on t'terraces and disgracing me in front of ivverybody. I don't want to hear none o' that "Good show, chaps" or "Play the game, you cads" while you're wit' me. If yer want to shout, shout proper.'

The crowd certainly shouted proper. Leeds were playing Wigan and bloodstreams were being stirred by ancient enmities going back to the Wars of the Roses. But, although there were twenty-seven people running around the field of play, the spectators seemed vocally interested in only three of them – Lewis Jones of Leeds, Billy Boston of Wigan, and the referee. If any Lancastrian laid finger on our Lewis, the Leeds loiners bellowed for its owner's instant deportation. When any Yorkshire body obstructed the bulldozing progress of Billy, thousands of Lancashire voices demanded his eternal suspension. Both factions, however, made common feud against the referee, each greeting his every decision against their own team with biting sarcasm, aspersions on his eyesight and doubts that his parents were ever churched.

G

'By! . . . but what a lovely boot he's got!' bawled Mr. Micklethwaite as Lewis Jones punted fifty yards to drop the ball a foot within the touchline before it ran neatly off. 'There's some skill in touch-kicking up here, lad. Got to bounce before it goes in. Not like your game where any daft ox can belt t'ball over t'stand whenever he can't think of owt else to do wi' it. There's no skill in that galumphing, is there now?'

'Nor in that kick by thi Lewis Jones,' said a near-by Wigan supporter, wearing a red and white beret and nose to match. 'Just a reight lucky bounce ower t'line.'

'Lucky?' boomed Mr. Micklethwaite. 'Nivver been a kicker like him in t'whole history o' Rugby League. I've nivver seen your Billy Boston boot t'ball ten yards in all my life.'

'Allus too busy scoring tries is our Billy . . . There he goes again! Get stuck into 'em, Billy.'

Which exhortation Billy forthwith obeyed, leaving three recumbent opponents to mark his passage before the full Yorkshire rearguard came across and rolled him into touch.

'In your game,' said Mr. Micklethwaite to me, 'you'd be having a line-out now. Curse o' t'Union, are line-outs. Half t'ruddy match spent wi' t'forwards lepping up and down like our Nancy's netball. You'd do better to tek a scrum and have done wi' it, right away.'

'But you don't even have proper scrums. Look at them now! . . . Just pile in anyhow, scrumhalf bounces the ball off somebody's foot and away they go.'

'You'll nivver mek no sense of scrums not if you lay down five hundred rules. Best thing to do is to get t'scrum over as quick as you can and get t'ball moving down t'line. Not keep sixteen grown men playing knockheads for ten minutes at a time. I've seen Union internationals on t'telly

that by t'time you've taken line-outs and scrums out o'
t'eighty minutes, all you get is a quarter of an hour of open
Rugby for your licence money.'

'I must confess,' I said, 'that, compared with your game,
we do seem to spend a lot of time with the ball doing
nothing.'

'You've too many men on the field, and all. Wi' fifteen
a side, there's so many in defence that ivverbody's bound
to keep getting clogged up. Cut it down to thirteen like
us, lad, and give your runners a chance to move. And
any road, if I had my way I'd cut our teams down to
twelve.'

'Tha'd do better wi' twelve today,' broke in the candy-
topped lad from Wigan. 'That Lewis Jones o' thine has
just knocked on again. Tha'd stand more chance o' winning
wi'out him.'

'Give over blethering,' retorted Mr. Micklethwaite. 'He's t'greatest all-rounder in t'game . . . Look at him just go! He left your Billy Boston standing like he were marble statue in t'City Square. You could do wi' leaving that

Billy behind in Lancasheer to see that t'hot-pot don't boil over and play Gracie Fields instead.'

'Aye, and our Gracie'd mek rings round thi Lewis Jones. He's past it, lad. Tha can see t'owld gaffer's lost all his hair.'

'That's just stupid, my man,' I remonstrated. 'Many fine athletes have gone prematurely bald. Look at Billy Bevan and . . .'

'And look at thi, too. Tha's only getting thi dander up

and talking all Oxford and Cambridge because tha's right thin on top thi'sen.'

'Tek no notice of him, lad,' said Mr. Micklethwaite, 'Happen he's got to leave at half-time to get back

into his cage as t'Missing Link on t'Golden Mile in Blackpool.'

'And only ruddy daft Yorkshiremen like thi two and Lewis Jones on Wakes Week as are mug enough to pay half-crown to see me.'

As he uttered the dreadful words, 'ruddy daft Yorkshiremen', a strange north-country stiffening seemed to creep up my backbone. My adrenalin-pumps went over to full pressure, my blood boiled with new patriotism, and my left hand shot out of its own volition to give Lancashire a warning shove in the chest.

'Not so much of the ruddy daft Yorkshiremen, lad,' I growled, 'or happen they'll have to be sending thi big Billy Boston up here to carry tha down to t'ambulance men. I know it's all t'rain on thi side o' t'Pennines as gives all thi Lancashire louts watter on t'brain, but if tha says owt else mawngy about Yorkshiremen, I'll bray tha one as'll gi' tha wedding bells in thi ears all t'way back to Wigan Pier.'

'Watter on t'brain, is it?' grated Wigan, squaring up in a stance reminiscent of John L. Sullivan. 'Tha'll need Lewis Jones wi' brush and pan to sweep up t'pieces when I've done wi' thi. Put 'em up, tha toffy-nosed tyke, and I'll stretch thi out on t'Ilkley Moor for good and all.'

Wigan came on looking so bony-fisted and spitefully Lancastrian that I was quite relieved when two of his mates stepped between us and Mr. Micklethwaite grabbed my arm.

'Hold on, lad!' he said as he led me away to the other end of the terrace. 'What the devil's come over you? He weren't running down your county. He nivver said nowt sarcastic about Hampsheer. You're only a Southerner, after all, and you've no right to go round standing up for Yorkshire.'

No more right, I then realized, than had the two brilliant causes of all the trouble and strife, those chosen county champions in that Rugby League War of the Roses, Billy Boston for Lancashire and Lewis Jones for Yorkshire, who were both born and bred Welshmen, look you, bach.

□ □

CHAPTER 15

THE ACCOLADE

A S WE WALKED TOGETHER out of the Headingley
ground after the match with Wigan was over,
Mr. Micklethwaite became wrapped in a cloud of
contemplative silence. He made no reply to my newly-
minted opinions about Rugby League tactics, but kept
looking at me sideways every now and again, like a farmer
weighing up the quality of a cow without betraying his
interest to its owner. He ruminated all the way down the
clinker-path and didn't speak a word until we were queuing
for the bus in Kirkstall Lane.

'Tell me, lad,' he suddenly said. 'Just how long have
you been up north now?'

'It'll be exactly a year on Monday.'

'A year, eh? I must say you've made it seem longer for
some of us.'

Silence set in again during the bus-journey, broken only
by the occasional sound of my seat-mate sucking a tooth in
judicial consideration. He seemed to come to some sort of a

decision as we got off at our stop and prepared to proceed our separate ways home.

'Right, lad,' he said. 'I think t'time's as ripe now as it's ivver likely to be. Could you come and have a drink with me and Enoch and a few of t'lads at my local on Tuesday?'

'I'd like to,' I said. 'Thank you very much.'

'Good. Then we'll say half past eight. And don't go knocking no more Lancashiremen about in between.'

At half past eight on Tuesday when I entered the Smoke-Room, it was already standing room only. Mr. Micklethwaite beckoned me to a vacant chair that he'd thoughtfully reserved at his table. As I sat down he tapped with his tankard and the gentlemen of the Smoke-Room murmured into silence.

'Best of order, please, gentlemen,' he said. 'And we'll get on wi' t'business. As you all know, I've asked this lad, my deputy at t'factory, round here this evening because he's now been resident in Yorkshire for a year and a day.'

A little applause ruffled around the room.

'Although, when I first set eyes on him twelve months ago, I can't say as how I ivver thought he'd last more nor five minutes up here.'

'He come into Josiah's office,' interpolated Mr. Enoch Arkengarth, 'carrying a bloody oomber-ella.'

The bar became inhabited by bitterns as shocked lips boomed, 'Oomber-ella . . . oomber-ella . . .' off the sounding-board of the nicotine-enamelled ceiling.

'But I don't carry it any more,' I explained hastily. 'It kept blowing inside-out every time I came round a corner on to Headrow and hit the trade-winds.'

'He came up from London, gentlemen, a right proper Southerner,' continued the chairman. 'He wore a black bowler-hat under that bloody oomber-ella, thought that cricket were only a game, and grew mint in his garden. He could neither understand the King's English when it were spoken to him nor express himself so's civilized folk could mek out what t'hell he were on about.'

'Come in here one night,' said Albert the barman, 'and asked for a pint o' mild and bitter.'

Heads wagged and jowls quivered as the company relished the comic memory.

'He were in favour of bringing live females into pubs, afraid to say boo to a shopkeeper, and content to be twisted daft wi'out mekking a mouse-squeak after value for his brass. T'poor lad were addicted to wimmin's work and he cleaned t'winders, papered t'walls and got t'coal in whenever his missus flicked her little finger at him. There was nowt fancy-dandy he wouldn't wear and nowt lady-fingered he wouldn't do. As I said, gentlemen, he were a Southerner o' t'first watter and nobody nivver got farther South than he were wi'out crossing t'ruddy Channel.'

'Aye,' said Mr. Crowther, the ironmonger, 'he used to come into my shop for nails and stuff when he were trying to bodge up that house old Postlethwaite lumbered on him, and he'd not have said owt but "Thank you very much" if tha'd short-changed him for ten bob and give him all t'crooked panel pins.'

'You don't surprise me, Joshua,' said Mr. Micklethwaite, 'and there were times early on when I reckoned we'd have to give him up as a bad job and send him C.O.D. back to London. But I'm happy to say, gentlemen, that during the last six months, t'lad has tekken a real turn for the better. T'penny seems to have dropped, t'light has broken through, and he's realized, at last, that t'only proper way for a self-respecting man to live in this world is to be a Yorkshire-man.'

The company banged the table with their glasses in agreement and delivered themselves of a symbolic, elastic-vowelled Amen.

'At t'factory, he don't seem so keen on yammer-yammer-yammering all day long and he's started to spend a bit more time thinking wi' his trap shut before laying down t'law. And when he does talk these days, he gets a bit of chest into his voice so's t'men can hear him on t'other side o' t'loading-yard. He's been up t'Three Peaks, along t'Lyke Wake Walk and down High Street, Pudsey, on wet Saturday night. All t'mint in his garden has died of rust and his missus complained to me last weekend that though she's been nagging him till laryngitis set in, she just can't get him to lay a single hair of his emulsion-brush on t'back bedroom ceiling.'

'And I saw him,' volunteered Mr. Crowther, 'last Friday fortnight, tek five lemons back to Birkenshaw the greengrocer because they weren't sour enough.'

'He came in here t'other day,' said Albert the barman, 'shuded t'pint that guv'nor gi' him back across t'bar and said, "If I wanted a two-inch snow-white collar on my pint, I'd have gone round to t'laundry, so let's see tha fill t'glass up wi' bitter."'

'I were behind him in t'queue for evening papers at end o' t'cricket season,' offered Mr. Arkengarth, 'and heerd him laying into Charlie the newsboy because he weren't shouting "Hampsheer tek t'Championship" loud enough for his lordship's taste. I nigh on missed my bus home before Charlie had got t'decibels up to his satisfaction.'

'Thank you, gentlemen,' said Mr. Micklethwaite, 'for your supporting evidence. And when I conclude by telling you that at t'League match at Headingley last Saturday I had all on to stop him braying the ears off a feller from

Wigan as were running down Yorkshire, I feel confident
that you will wish me to proceed forthwith to the formal
presentation.'

'Aye . . .' everybody rumbled. 'Aye . . . we do and all.'

Mr. Micklethwaite rose to his feet and beckoned me to
do likewise.

'It gives me great pleasure, lad,' he said ceremonially,
'particularly when I recall the pitiful state of Southern
degradation you were in twelve months ago, to congratu-
late you on having successfully completed your first year
as an Apprentice Yorkshireman, and to present you on
behalf of the assembled company with these traditional
tokens of primary graduation.'

From under the table he produced a brown-paper bag
and a baking-tin. The former contained a noble russet-and-
grey flat cap and a plastic white rose, and the latter, a
square foot of golden Yorkshire pudding. With all the
solemnity of an archbishop at coronation, he placed the
cap on my head, the rose in my left hand, and the pudding
in my right.

'Hear all, see all, say nowt,' he intoned. 'Eat all, drink all,
pay nowt. And if tha does owt for nowt, do it for thisen . . .
I now declare tha, lad, a passed-out First Year Apprentice
Yorkshireman and authorize tha to continue your residence
in t'Premier County.'

'You mean . . .' I asked, my voice trembling at the sudden
honour, the flower quivering and the pudding shaking in
my grasp, 'D'you mean that I can now become a Yorkshireman?'

'Aye, lad,' Mr. Micklethwaite said as the company gave
out with verse and chorus of 'On Ilkley Moor Baht 'At'.
'Happen tha can . . . If tha serves t'remaining twenty-four
years o' thi Apprenticeship satisfactorily.'